W9-BMD-939

Starting and Running a
Nonprofit Organization
second edition

Starting and Running a Nonprofit Organization

second edition

Joan M. Hummel

Revised by the Center for Nonprofit Management
Graduate School of Business
University of St. Thomas

University of Minnesota Press
Minneapolis
London

Copyright 1980, 1996 by the Regents of the University of Minnesota

All rights reserved. No part of this publication may be reproduced, stored in a retrieval system, or transmitted, in any form or by any means, electronic, mechanical, photocopying, recording, or otherwise, without the prior written permission of the publisher.

Published by the University of Minnesota Press
111 Third Avenue South, Suite 290
Minneapolis, MN 55401-2520
http://www.upress.umn.edu

Printed in the United States of America on acid-free paper

Sixth printing, 2004

Library of Congress Cataloging-in-Publication Data
Hummel, Joan M.
       Starting and running a nonprofit organization / Joan M. Hummel. —
2nd ed. / Revised by the Center for Nonprofit Management, Graduate
School of Business, University of St. Thomas.
          p.   cm.
       "Revised by the Center for Nonprofit Management, Graduate School
of Business, University of St. Thomas."
       Includes bibliographical references and index.
       ISBN 0-8166-2777-0 (pbk.)
       1. Nonprofit organizations—Management.   2. New business
enterprises—Management.   I. University of St. Thomas. Center for
Nonprofit Management.   II. Title.
       HD62.6.H85   1996
       658'.048—dc20   95-53699

The University of Minnesota is an equal-opportunity educator and employer.

Contents

Thanks . . .

To Ricky Littlefield, director of the Center for Nonprofit Management, who guided the preparation of this revised edition, and to Kent Shamblin of the Center, who edited the text and developed additional material to reflect the numerous changes in laws, regulations, and management practices that have occurred since the original edition was published in 1980.

A number of other people have been instrumental in determining what needed to be updated or added to the book:

- Barbara Davis, executive director, Resources and Counseling for the Arts, St. Paul
- Barbara Beltrand, certified public accountant and nonprofit accounting specialist, St. Paul
- Ann Howden, financial consultant, The Stevens Group, St. Paul
- Pat Plunkett, partner, Moore, Costello & Hart, St. Paul
- The staff of MAP for Nonprofits, St. Paul.

We also add our thanks to those who reviewed all or portions of the revised manuscript for accuracy and clarity, as well as for its value to those who are starting and running nonprofit organizations!

- Edward Gill, CPA, chief financial officer, Minnesota Orchestra Association, Minneapolis
- Ellie Hands, founding executive director, Minnesota Head Injury Association, St. Paul

- Pam Harris, attorney, Rider, Bennett, Egan & Arundel, Minneapolis
- Jackie Hill, director of human resources, Amherst H. Wilder Foundation, St. Paul
- Clareen Menzies, development coordinator, Institute on Black Chemical Abuse, Minneapolis
- Michael F. Sullivan, Ph.D., vice president, business affairs, University of St. Thomas, St. Paul
- James V. Toscano, executive vice president, Institute for Research and Education, HealthSystem Minnesota, St. Louis Park

Also, a special thanks to the former staff and board members of Enablers, Inc., who advised and assisted in the development of the first edition of this book, especially Terri Barreiro, Douglas Johnson, David Nelson, and Albert Veranth. Enablers, Inc., was an organization that helped many nonprofits get off the ground in the Minneapolis-St. Paul area during the 1970s.

About This Revised Edition of *Starting and Running a Nonprofit Organization*

This handbook is for people who are forming new nonprofits, thinking about converting an informal, grassroots group to tax-exempt status, reorganizing an existing agency, or in the early stages of managing a nonprofit. It provides practical and basic how-to information for the small nonprofit.

When the original edition of this handbook was produced in 1980, little was available in a single, simple book form concerning the legal, tax, organizational, and other issues involved in managing even a small nonprofit. There was almost nothing generally available of much use to people starting up a nonprofit. Today, numerous books are published on nonprofit management, but *Starting and Running a Nonprofit Organization* remains unique as a compact guide for the new or reorganized small nonprofit.

Most of the information provided here will be useful to any nonprofit practitioner in any state. Where regulations or other legal requirements vary by state, the Minnesota law is used as an example, but the handbook can be used as a tool to research the laws that apply to nonprofits in other states. When tax laws and reporting requirements apply differently to the thirty various types of nonprofits, this handbook focuses on charitable nonprofits, often called "501(c)(3)s" because of the applicable IRS tax code chapter.

At the end of this book are two short sections for the nonprofit practitioner interested in and willing and able to invest in acquiring additional knowledge. The first lists sources for assistance and management development; the second is a bibliography of some of the available publications on nonprofit management.

Introduction

The French politician Alexis de Tocqueville wrote about 160 years ago that "Americans are forever forming associations." Today, that remains a strong characteristic of our society, and a great many critical services are provided to the American public by nonprofit associations, in addition to those provided by governments and businesses.

Throughout the country, nonprofit organizations provide needed services to children, other young people, elder adults, the mentally and physically differently abled, and other socially or economically disadvantaged people. They promote the arts. They advocate for the rights of people in our nation's wide range of human diversity and focus attention on threats to the environment, the rights of consumers, and other critical interests of our society. They work and volunteer in support of many religious faiths and organizations. They foster the development of professionals in a variety of fields. They provide recreational and educational opportunities. And there are a variety of civic associations in almost every city and town.

The number of nonprofit organizations in the United States increases each year. Among this growth is a new wave of grassroots organizations—young, often struggling groups put together by members of a community who have an issue on their minds and who, most often, have little or no experience in agency development and very little money in their pockets. The range of concerns of these grassroots groups is enormous.

An organization develops from a seed—a common concern, a critical issue, a central purpose, an individual's passion. If this seed interests enough people, including potential contributors who share the passion, a group of some sort forms. Individuals who have a common concern and want to do something about it begin meeting, talking, and planning their directions. One direction such a group may take is to form an organization with a name, identity, and purpose, and possibly a membership or staff. The most common form an organization of this nature can take is that of a nonprofit corporation. (The benefits derived from this form of organization are discussed in the chapter on legal aspects.)

But there are other directions to consider. There may be a better way to achieve the group's goals than by formalizing into yet another nonprofit organization that will be subject to various and increasing state and federal regulations, required financial reporting, competitive fund raising, the time-consuming establishment and operation of a formal board of directors, and the like. If a group does not need to raise much, if any, money to achieve its purpose, it may be able to function as a loosely knit association. If the group is uncertain about the need to form a permanent organization, it might find an established nonprofit sympathetic to its "cause" that will act as a "foster parent" on a temporary basis. This could include providing office space and a telephone. In some cases, the established nonprofit might agree to serve as a "fiscal agent" for any money the group raises. If a group is concerned that a certain type of service should be made available to a community, it could work with an existing organization in the same service area to develop the specific type of program needed. Or the group might find that a neighboring community has the type of organization needed and try to persuade that organization to open a branch in its community.

After considering these options, a group may still decide that it should establish a separate, legal identity to accomplish its mission and secure the legal and other advantages that incorporation offers. It may form a nonprofit corporation regardless of whether it has paid staff or an office, offers established programs to the public, or solicits fees from its participants.

Many small nonprofits are managed entirely by unpaid volunteers. This may be a temporary measure in the formative stages of the new organization, with an executive director and other staff added as the group expands and obtains the necessary funds, or it may be a permanent arrangement. However, most direct service agencies need paid staff in order to serve their clientele. When considering these alternative ways to operate, a group should keep in mind that the form it decides is most feasible in the organization's infancy does not have to be permanent. Organizations can change and grow and develop different ways of functioning as necessary.

A group needs more than an issue, a goal, or a mission to make something happen. It needs a well-thought-out program, a sound financial base, an effective staff (paid or volunteer) and board of directors, and good community relations. These are areas of management expertise that can be developed by grassroots organizers with time, effort, and help from others.

This book will serve as an introduction to the basic concepts and skills of agency planning and development. Because nonprofit organizations must rely on limited resources, their leaders should learn to develop their human and monetary assets to the fullest. Many worthwhile and needed programs ultimately fail to reach their goals because they were not put together well; their organizational skeletons were too weak to carry the weight. In the end, it is the client and the community who are affected most by such failures. The tradition of community service will be carried on by the newest crop of nonprofits if the roots they plant in their early stages are strong ones.

A Checklist of Things to Be Done When Starting a Nonprofit Organization

This checklist is a summary of the key considerations and actions that the founders of a new nonprofit organization generally should consider. The sequence shown here will not always be the chronological way a new nonprofit develops, but this list can serve as a general guide for the development of your own checklist and target dates. Every item in this checklist is discussed in the chapters that follow.

1. Establish the charitable purpose of the anticipated program; research whether or not other nonprofits are engaged in the same program; consider if you need to incorporate or if you could partner with an existing nonprofit.
2. If you conclude you need to proceed with starting a new nonprofit, create a clear, succinct, written statement of mission (charitable purpose) and vision.
3. Recruit initial board of directors and source of legal expertise.
4. Determine state requirements for incorporation.
5. Draft articles of incorporation.
6. Draft bylaws.
7. Secure material for obtaining tax-exempt status.
8. Hold meeting of initial board; approve articles and bylaws; authorize tax-exempt filing; elect officers; agree on periodic meeting schedule; agree on committees; appoint board members to committees.
9. File articles of incorporation with state; determine annual reporting requirements, if any, in your state.

10. File application with the IRS for tax-exempt status.
11. After receipt of IRS tax-exempt status, file application for exemption from state income tax (if applicable and required in your state).
12. Determine if sales tax exemption can be secured in your state; if so, file application.
13. Develop strategic plan (or at least a tentative plan that will be revisited after a year of operation); secure board approval.
14. Develop one-year work plan for each program activity, including process to measure outcomes, and determine budget for each program.
15. Develop one-year organizational budget; secure board approval; seek start-up funding from board members and other key supporters.
16. Locate source of accounting expertise.
17. Establish accounting system and record-keeping procedures; open bank account.
18. Develop fund raising plan.
19. Apply for solicitation license from local city if required.
20. Apply for nonprofit mail permit (reduced rate for bulk mailings).
21. Develop and submit grant proposals; initiate fund raising from individual donors.
22. Recruit paid staff and/or volunteers as needed.
23. File employer registration with federal/state governments for income tax and FICA withholding (involves securing federal employer number).
24. Register with state unemployment insurance program per requirements of your state.
25. Determine office and equipment situation and secure appropriate facility.
26. Apply for property tax exemption, if applicable, with local tax assessor's office.
27. Secure liability insurance.
28. Secure insurance to cover any equipment and other property owned.
29. Develop personnel policies (if you have paid staff).
30. Hold orientation sessions for staff and volunteers.

31. Begin marketing program services to clientele.
32. Create and implement community relations plan.
33. Begin program activities.
34. Monitor client satisfaction with services.
35. Monitor expenses in relation to budget.
36. Evaluate outcomes of programs (may not be productive until after one year of experience).
37. Reassess validity of purpose, mission, vision, goals, and strategies (involve representatives of all constituencies); discuss with board; revise as needed (six months to one year after beginning operations).

Boards of Directors: "Behind Every Good Organization..."

Your program probably owes its existence to a creative spark that went off in the heads of a few concerned individuals who came up with a good idea—the original organizers of your program. Your organization will keep going, however, because this idea is nurtured and given the opportunity to develop, change, and expand by other groups of people, including your board of directors. The board of directors is legally, financially, and morally responsible for the operations and conduct of the nonprofit corporation.

The board should not be static. Its size, structure, and composition should respond to the evolving scope and needs of your organization. In the beginning, the initial organizers should seek out other people with the interest and skills necessary to help translate ideas into functioning services. If and when the organization incorporates, this group can serve as the initial board of directors. As the organization continues to develop, the composition of the board will likely need to change. In spite of the inevitable (and appropriate) turnover in board membership, the board provides continuity for the nonprofit corporation.

What Does the Board of Directors Do?

What do the staff and the board need to understand about the functions of the board of directors? First, you need to understand that the board is charged with a "governing" role. Boards are fiduciaries of nonprofit corporations. *Fiduciaries* is a term not often heard in casual conversation, but what it means is important—fiduciaries stand in a special relation of legal trust to others. Thus, the board of a nonprofit is answerable to the agency's members, if any, and to the government agencies that regulate and monitor nonprofit corporations on behalf of the community, for at least two duties:

1. *Duty of care:* being diligent and acting prudently as a director overseeing the affairs of the nonprofit. This doesn't mean a director is expected to foresee every potential problem or prevent any wrongdoing that could occur, although in some states, the duty is that of a trustee, a very high standard requiring a duty of utmost care. In other states, the duty is that which a person of ordinary prudence would reasonably be expected to act under similar circumstances.
2. *Duty of loyalty:* acting in good faith and not allowing personal interests to override responsibility as a director.

Board members must give more than lip service to the serious responsibility they undertake when they agree to serve, because under the laws of every state they have certain legal duties and can incur liabilities for failure to meet those duties.

Second, everyone should agree that individual members of the board, *including the chair,* have no authority except as given by the board or as stated in the articles of incorporation or the bylaws. This is a legal limitation in some states.

Third, generally the board makes decisions only in meetings or through a proper "action in writing." Again, this is a legal limitation in some states. Generally, an action in writing must be unanimous.

In new, small nonprofits, board members also tend to act as cheerleaders for the organization's founders and staff. If there are only one or two employees or a part-time staff or no staff at all, the board may, in addition to its governing responsibilities, function as a "working" board. That is, members of the board may do some types of work that normally are, and should be, carried out by employees, such as bookkeeping and writing grant requests.

Finally, the board and the senior staff should understand that one of the most important duties of the board is to review the performance of the senior staff (the process may be delegated to a committee of the board); this includes replacing the senior staff person in charge of the organization when that is in the best interest of the organization.

The board generally assumes specific responsibilities in the areas described below.

Budget and Finance

The board is ultimately accountable for the responsible and prudent use of money and other assets. To meet this accountability, the board determines the organization's fiscal policies and internal control practices. The board also reviews and approves the budget, which generally is prepared by the staff, and reviews and approves the annual audit of the organization's financial condition, bookkeeping practices, and financial records.

Strategic and Annual Plans

The board works with management in developing the mission and vision of the organization. It should review and approve the strategic (long-range) direction and goals prepared by the staff. Boards often also choose to approve annual operating objectives and organizational priorities. In some organizations, a board committee may assist the staff in developing the strategic plan and, especially in small nonprofits, may also help work up the year-to-year objectives.

Fund Raising

Fund raising is not a legal responsibility of the board, but most nonprofits expect some or all of the board members to participate in fund raising activities, such as serving as the agency's contacts with certain potential funders. Board members usually are expected to make personal financial contributions to the organization at whatever level each finds comfortable. Even a modest donation is symbolically important.

Policy

The board reviews and approves the organization's operating policies, perhaps through various committees, that the staff proposes. (*Policies* are the rules or guidelines that provide the framework for the staff's decision making or actions; for example, "All checks larger than $500 must be signed by two people.") Sometimes boards, especially those of new or small nonprofits, will go beyond policies and insist on establishing procedures that spell out what steps must be taken and who must be included in certain internal processes, although generally procedures should be formulated by the staff and only reviewed by the appropriate board committees.

Human Resources

The board hires the executive director (or the chief staff person, whatever the title), evaluates his or her effectiveness, and removes him or her when performance is unsatisfactory. The board may determine the salary scales and benefits for the staff, especially if they have professional expertise that the staff does not, and may approve staff-developed personnel policies. (However, staff members who report to the executive director generally should be hired, fired, and evaluated by the executive director, who should also determine their individual compensation within the overall compensation policy approved by the board.)

Community Relationships

Most nonprofits exist to serve one or more specific communities. A community may be everyone within a geographic area, such as a neighborhood or entire city, or it may consist of an ethnic group or other particular segment of society. An organization's communities also include donors and government. The board is accountable to these communities for the effective and ethical performance of the organization. Too often, boards become concerned with how their organizations are interacting with their communities only when a crisis comes to board members' attention through the media.

Program Evaluation

Program evaluation is the process through which the actual outcomes of programs (the services the nonprofit exists to provide) are measured against specific objectives. This is a responsibility of the staff, but the board should be informed of evaluation results.

Board Development

Although the bylaws usually establish the structure of the board (officers, directors' terms, and ongoing committees), the board itself often determines how frequently it meets, sets the criteria and procedure to secure board members, appoints members of committees, and sets standards for its own self-evaluation. Unless the organization has members with voting rights, the board selects new board members.

Advising Staff

The board may offer administrative guidance to the staff, but this can often lead to micromanagement. The executive director is hired to get the things done that are consistent with the mission and the strategic direction set by the board. If he or she needs mentoring or could benefit from certain kinds of advice, a separate group of volunteers with that expertise or experiences might be set up.

Getting Organized

The board of directors must organize itself in a manner that allows its duties to be carried out in a timely and responsible way. The bylaws of your organization usually are the general rules that govern the organization and define the board's composition and structure (although bylaws are not legally required by some states). The rules should allow the board to be flexible enough to respond to the changing needs of the organization.

There is no one best model for a nonprofit board. The size of the board, types of committees, frequency of meetings, and other aspects of governance will vary according to the characteristics of different organizations.

Officers

The board selects one of its members to be the chair, who presides at meetings, keeps the group directed toward its goals, delegates responsibility for tasks to other members or committees, and serves as the primary contact between the board and the executive director and other staff. The chair is responsible for keeping the group of directors functioning effectively and efficiently.

Other officers typically designated in bylaws include a vice chair (who fills in for the chair as needed) and perhaps a treasurer (who has general responsibility for the agency's funds and accounts, but this role can and probably should be delegated to staff). Sometimes a director is designated as secretary, responsible for the written records of the board, including the minutes of meetings, but usually the secretary's responsibilities are best assigned to a staff member, if feasible (the minutes may get done faster that way, unless the staff member has too heavy a workload).

Committees

Dividing board work by committees is the most effective means of governance for many organizations, as well as a way to make sure board members feel well utilized. *Committees have only the authority that is specifically given to them by the bylaws or the board.* If your board is small, it may prefer to deal as a body with the business of the corporation, with no need for committee work. But if your board has a dozen or more members, it may choose to divide its major responsibilities among standing (ongoing) committees, which report to the board as a whole. Board members with interest and expertise in specific areas are appointed, generally by the board's chair, to serve on standing committees. In some states, all committee members must be members of the board. In other states, the board is permitted to appoint other people to committees, which it may want to do to acquire special expertise, spread the major time commitments required among more people, or involve potential candidates for future board membership.

Even if your organization chooses not to develop an extensive committee structure, it may have an *executive committee*. Typically, an executive committee is composed of the officers of the corporation and the chairs of key board committees. An executive committee may fulfill a variety of roles, and it is essential that the bylaws clearly define these roles.

For example, an executive committee could be given decision-making authority in the by-laws to act on urgent business that arises during the periods between board meetings. The bylaws might authorize the board to delegate additional authority to the executive committee, although care should be taken that the full board does not become a "rubber stamp" or a group that meets infrequently and does not fulfill a normal governance role.

If the bylaws provide for the committee to carry out certain duties but state that these are "subject to the approval of the board," the executive committee is only advisory. As an adviser, an executive committee can be responsible for planning other board activities and for developing the agendas of board meetings. If there are no other committees, the executive committee may take on the functions that otherwise would be handled by standing committees.

Your organization should determine its committee structure and the powers of committees carefully, keeping in mind the size of the board, the amount of time board members are able or willing to commit, and the needs of the organization. A relatively young agency may start with no committee structure or only one or two committees, and add more committees as it develops. In a fully developed board committee structure, which many new and small nonprofits will not find necessary, the standing committees generally correspond to the various areas of the board's responsibilities, outlined earlier in this chapter.

The *finance committee* monitors fiscal operations, assists the executive director in developing an annual budget, and assures that an audit is performed annually. It may also be responsible for developing and overseeing a fund raising plan (or this may be assigned to a *development committee*).

The *nominating committee* recommends individuals to serve as board members. It may also be assigned the broader role of board development. This would include recommending the criteria for selecting new board members (otherwise, the board as a whole should develop the criteria), providing orientation to new members (although the chair and executive director may fill this role), and reviewing the participation and performance of current members.

The *human resources committee* reviews personnel needs, determines the schedules of salaries and benefits, and develops personnel policies. If the board wants to provide a grievance review body for staff, this committee could be designated to serve that role.

A *community relations committee*, which ideally would include people with public relations expertise, may be established to work with the staff in disseminating information about the organization to its different publics through the media and by other means.

A *program committee* of volunteers may be useful to advise the staff in service delivery activities, recommend service delivery policies, monitor the agency's services, and provide the board with detailed information regarding the effectiveness of these services.

As an alternative (or addition) to standing committees, many boards utilize temporary committees, which are formed to do one project and then disbanded. For example, a special committee may be formed in the absence of a human resources committee to search for a new executive director and disbanded after the position is filled. Or a committee could be formed to work with staff on a new strategic plan.

Communications

Regular channels of communication must be set up among board members and between the board and the staff. The most common of these communication channels, of course, are periodic board meetings. Small and active boards tend to have monthly meetings. Larger boards may meet only quarterly to deal with major issues, while committees of board members work on organizational concerns between the quarterly board meetings. Most state laws do not require even one meeting a year, but it is a matter of good governance for board meetings to be held at least four times a year. Your organization must determine a meeting schedule (including where to meet, for how long, and what time of the day) that suits its needs and responsibilities and that operates within the time constraints of its board members.

The minutes of board meetings are very important, because they function as legal records of a nonprofit corporation. In general, minutes should be shorter rather than longer, but all controversial or potentially controversial issues, major litigation, and matters involving substantial amounts of money should be raised at meetings of the board, with the minutes noting that issues were discussed and recording any decisions made. Minutes are subject to review by financial auditors, in some legal matters, and by the IRS in connection with any audit of compliance with tax-exemption conditions. Executive committee meetings should also be recorded in minutes. Action items recorded in the minutes should include who has the authority to carry out the action.

Board meetings should provide sufficient opportunity for the exchange of opinions and proposed actions between management and the board members.

The chair of the board should meet regularly with the executive director, and should play a major role in keeping communication channels open and effective. He or she should ensure that (1) board members clearly understand the strategies and goals of the agency and their roles in the organization's governance; (2) meetings that are called are truly necessary and deal with important matters; (3) agendas and meeting notices are sent well in advance of meetings, accurate minutes are prepared soon after meetings occur, and these minutes are included in materials sent to the board; and (4) the staff and board have opportunities to interact.

The executive director also is responsible for assuring that the organization's official documents are safeguarded and kept at one location. He or she should never allow them to become scattered among various board members' personal files.

Who Is on the Board?

How Many Members Should Constitute a Board?

State laws may establish the minimum size of a board for a nonprofit organization. Check with your secretary of state's office regarding any requirements for a nonprofit corporation in your state.

The best size for your board depends on the needs of your organization. The most important consideration is that it be able to work efficiently and effectively. Most boards probably function best with a dozen or so members, and a new, small nonprofit might function better with only a half dozen or so. Unfortunately, efficiency and even effectiveness sometimes give way to the perceived need to include representatives of all constituencies. Some or all of this need may be met by forming a special advisory group to the executive director that has no legal responsibilities and no decision-making authority.

Who Should Be on the Board?

Ideally, the composition of the board should be varied enough to provide variety in areas of expertise, perspective, and human diversity. Board members should be selected according to what they can provide to your organization, especially in the following areas:

- *Competence:* This is the number-one priority. Board members should be capable of making sound governance decisions and of understanding basic financial reports. Special competencies may also be included, such as in the areas of finance, general management, law, and public relations. Competence in the organization's program areas may also be desirable.
- *Bridge to constituencies:* Members of the target population of the program and other stakeholders may be considered.
- *Community leadership:* Some members of the board could be leaders in the community, have access to resources, and/or possess affiliations with other organizations of importance to your own.
- *Shared goals:* Board members should share the mission and vision of the organization and bring a commitment to see the organization succeed.

Other factors to consider in the composition of the board include the goal of balance in human diversity, including diversity of age, gender, and race. Some organizations develop formal selection criteria for board members designed to ensure that certain proportions of the board represent specific groups. Such criteria may also assure that the board includes a diverse representation of skills and viewpoints.

It is tempting to try to add some "letterhead heavies" to your board—people who occupy prominent public positions in the community but aren't expected to do any actual work or attend board meetings. The theory is that their names on your letterhead or their signatures on your letters make it easier to raise funds from some foundations and corporations. However, prominent names on a letterhead seldom impress sophisticated donors, and committed directors may resent such never-seen members.

What You Should Look for in a Board Member

Your first priority in looking for board members should be to find people with a sincere interest in the work of the organization, a commitment to its goals, a willingness to ask questions, the ability to offer constructive criticism, and an understanding of the difference between making suggestions to staff and taking over their management prerogatives. Along with these traits, you want people with enough expertise, experience, and good judgment to help keep the organization's mission and strategic decisions consistent with its charitable purpose, so it can achieve its goals.

None of the above qualifications will mean a thing, however, unless your directors have the time, dependability, and energy required to attend meetings and otherwise serve the organization well.

Finally, you should consider the likely ability of your candidates to work well with the other directors.

How Do You Invite Someone to Join Your Board?

Your initial contact with a potential board member is quite important. You want this individual to know what is exciting and interesting about your organization. You want him or her to conclude that serving on your board is worthwhile. If there is someone on your board who knows the person you are considering, that board member is the best person to contact the potential member. Otherwise, the chair or another board member should be asked to interview each potential member.

The initial meeting, which might be over breakfast or lunch, or in another social setting, should allow enough time for a detailed discussion of your organization and the role of board members. When discussing board involvement with potential members, you should speak clearly about why they were selected; in what capacity they will serve; what skills and viewpoints you want them to contribute; the committee work they will be expected to do; the amount of time they can expect to be involved in meetings and other activities; the length of their terms on the board; the possible cost to them as board members, such as for lunches, travel, and time away from work; and any expectation of personal financial contributions. You should also try to ascertain whether or not potential board members have any conflicts of interest (any business or other relationships that could affect their ability to serve your organization's interests).

In exchange, you should ask prospective board members what they want to contribute to your organization and how their participation can be easily and best utilized by your organization. Remember that board members need rewards too, and consider what your organization can give to its board members, such as the satisfaction of serving the community, social contacts, and experience in policy making, fund raising, and other aspects of the agency.

Prospective members should not be rushed for answers at the initial meeting; rather, you should encourage them to take some time to think about your invitation. New board members who are well informed about the organization, including its problems and opportunities, and about their own expected role are more likely to participate well and be effective board members.

Getting Oriented

In order for board members to function effectively, they must first have a thorough understanding of the organization they serve. New members, as individuals or as a group, should be introduced to the program by current board members or staff. This introduction should include information about the community needs your organization serves; its programs; its strategic goals, strategies, and philosophy; and its sources of operating funds. You should also provide the minutes of recent board meetings so new members can review the issues, and decisions, the board has addressed. Include a tour of your facility and an introduction to staff members.

Each new board member should be given a file that includes the organization's mission statement; statement of goals; budget; list of funding sources; bylaws; organizational chart; the names, addresses, and phone numbers of the board members and senior staff; and a list of current board committee assignments. Any brochures or major reports recently issued or grant proposals pending could also provide useful information for new board members. You should also discuss with new board members any indemnification clause in your bylaws (the organization indemnifies board members for legal expense and judgments in case of lawsuits alleging negligence; in some states, they must be indemnified unless the bylaws say otherwise). The purchase of directors and officers liability insurance is strongly recommended. Knowledgeable community and business leaders often will decline to join a board that has no "D&O" coverage.

To achieve a diverse, representative board, you may recruit board members with little or no background in management or governance processes. Representatives of your client group are especially likely to lack this expertise. In such cases, you should provide special training to enable these members to contribute fully. This training should include lessons in group-process skills, parliamentary procedure, how to read and understand a budget, and legal requirements for nonprofit corporations. Orientation programs for new board members and annual board/staff retreats provide good opportunities to inform board members about the organization's activities and issues.

Effective boards of directors are not developed overnight. They must be carefully nurtured and maintained. The contributions that a committed and skilled board can make to your organization are well worth the preparation and other hard work, the occasional conflicts, the periodic tedium, and the frustrations that are common even among the most "together" of boards.

Bylaws: Playing by the Rules

Bylaws are the rule book for a nonprofit corporation. They govern most of the internal affairs of your organization. They determine who has power and how that power works. They give structure to your organization, help prevent conflicts and disagreements, and can protect against the misuse of funds.

Bylaws outline how your board of directors will operate; they specify the size of the board, the selection and tenure of board members, the number of board meetings, the numbers of officers and committees, the financial and legal procedures, and the purpose of the organization.

Bylaws should be tailored to meet the needs of *your* organization. The model provisions offered in this chapter can be helpful, but you should not simply adopt a set of bylaws formulated by someone else. Decide how you want your own organization to function. Remember that these rules may not be appropriate forever; your bylaws should outline steps by which they can be revised when it becomes necessary or desirable.

If you incorporate (see the next chapter), some of what otherwise would be in your bylaws will be included in your articles of incorporation; this material need not be duplicated in the bylaws.

The following questionnaire outlines the decisions you will need to make about what will be in your bylaws. For each question, a sample bylaw provision is provided, but you should remember that this is only an example. You should have your bylaws reviewed by an attorney to ensure that they meet the legal requirements of your state. Although state laws do not necessarily require that you address all of the following items, generally it is wise to include them.

Chapter-by-Chapter Bylaws Guide

(The headings shown in all capital letters below may be used as the chapter titles in your bylaws, unless your state requires a different format.)

I. What is the PURPOSE of the organization?

Example: *The primary purpose of this organization is exclusively religious, charitable, scientific, literary, or educational within the meaning of Section 501(c)(3) of the Internal Revenue Code of 1986 or such other provisions of state or federal law as may from time to time be applicable. The specific purposes are to* (outline your organization's specific purposes or services to be provided).

II. Where will be the location of the organization (REGISTERED OFFICE)?

Example: *The registered office shall be located at* (address) *unless otherwise established by the board of directors.*

III. Will the organization have MEMBERS?

There is a distinction between members of an organization and members of its board of directors. State rules vary as to whether a nonprofit is required to have members. Sometimes a state will not require members generally, but will carve out exceptions. For example, Minnesota formerly required members, but now does not, *except* that charitable organizations licensed to conduct "charitable gambling" must have at least fifteen active members.

If a nonprofit has members, they generally meet only once a year. In most nonprofits, members do not have to be given any powers. There may be exceptions in your state. Some nonprofits provide for the members to elect the board of directors; adopt or revise bylaws; and approve mergers, dissolutions, and sale of assets. In other nonprofits, members are simply the people who make annual contributions. (If allowed by state law, bylaws should make it clear that these types of members are not legal members with voting rights.)

If the organization will not have members, the bylaws should specifically state that there are no members. If the founders of a nonprofit conclude there is a value to having members, the following questions should be addressed:

1. What are the qualifications for membership?

Example: *The membership of this corporation shall be open to all individuals, persons, corporations, proprietorships, associations, partnerships, and clubs interested in the promotion of the objectives and purposes of this corporation and who are deemed qualified for membership under the terms established by the board of directors and have met all conditions for membership* (such as paying dues).

(You may also establish classes of membership, e.g., *individual persons and families* and *corporate members*, each paying different dues or fees and/or each having different rights and duties.)

2. What is the length of membership?

Example: *Membership shall terminate at the end of the term as established by the board of directors and may not otherwise be terminated or suspended other than for nonpayment of dues or fees fixed by the board of directors except where the member is given not less than fifteen days' written notice and reasons and the member is given an opportunity to be heard orally or in writing. A terminated or suspended member may be reinstated by action of the board of directors.* (Note: This provision for termination would be permitted under some state laws, but rules vary from state to state.)

3. Powers: What can the members decide, if anything?

Example: *Members are not entitled to vote.*

Or: *Members shall approve any changes to the bylaws and all mergers.*

4. Meetings: What is the least number of meetings that will be held during a year; who can call the meeting; what advance notice is required; how many members must be present to conduct business; will Robert's Rules of Order or Sturgis parliamentary rules prevail (it is advisable to designate a specific set of rules); and can members vote by proxy? (You should meet at least once a year. Don't set a quorum that will be difficult to reach without extraordinary efforts; on the other hand, some states do not allow such a low number that only a few attendees will satisfy it.)

Example: *An annual meeting shall be held at a date, time, and place determined by the board of directors, with written notice to each member provided at least fifteen days in advance of the meeting* (some states specify the minimum). *An officer of the organization shall chair the meeting. A quorum shall consist of (?) members. Proxy votes are (are not) permitted. Robert's Rules of Order will govern motions, voting, and other conduct of the meeting.*

IV. What will be the structure of the BOARD OF DIRECTORS?

1. What will be the size of the board?

As noted in the chapter on the board of directors, the laws of your state may establish a minimum size. Otherwise, the best size depends on the needs of your particular organization. Most boards probably do well with a dozen or so members, but a new, small nonprofit may want to begin with a half dozen. The most important consideration should be the ability of the board to work efficiently and effectively.

Example: *The business and charitable affairs of the corporation will be managed under the direction of a board of directors comprising not fewer than six persons and not more than fifteen, as determined by the board.*

2. Who is eligible to be a member of the board of directors? If there are certain groups who should be represented or if there will be any "ex officio" directors, these should be indicated. (It is important to understand that ex officio board members are not "unofficial," "honorary," or "nonvoting." Rather, an ex officio director serves on the board because of his or her office, such as the chief staff officer, and has all of the rights of the other directors. Some nonprofits decide that the executive director should be a member ex officio; others conclude otherwise. There's no one right answer.)

Example: *At all times, not less than 25 percent of the directors shall be persons who represent (?). The executive director shall be a member of the board ex officio.*

3. How long do board members serve, and can they serve more than one term? The bylaws may also spell out the nominating process, or this could be left to the board to decide.

Example: *Directors shall be elected by the affirmative vote of a majority of the directors present at a duly held meeting of the board, except that no director shall vote for his/her own election, and shall serve for a term of three years each, but shall be so elected that approximately one-third are elected each year. A director may serve no more than two consecutive three-year terms.* (The incorporators, named in the articles of incorporation, can serve as the initial directors, who then elect the additional beginning directors.)

4. How are board members who resign during their terms replaced? Typically, the board elects replacements, unless it chooses to leave any positions vacant.

Example: *Should a director die, resign, or be removed, the board may elect a director to serve for the duration of the unexpired term.*

5. Can board members be removed from the board of directors before their terms are over? If so, how? Under what conditions? In most states, the board may not remove a director who was elected by the members.

Example: *A director may be removed from office, with or without cause, by an affirmative vote of a majority of the directors present at a duly called meeting, provided that not less than five days' and not more than thirty days' notice of such meeting, stating that removal of such director is to be on the agenda, shall be given to each director.*

6. Will board members be compensated for time, services, transportation, or other expenses? Generally, bylaws of nonprofits indicate that board members will not be paid for time and services. State laws governing incorporation may state whether or not such board members can receive monetary compensation.

Example: *No compensation shall be paid to any member of the board of directors for services as a member of the board, except that by resolution of the board, directors may be reimbursed for expenses incurred on behalf of the corporation.*

V. How are the MEETINGS OF THE BOARD OF DIRECTORS structured?

1. What is the minimum number of times the board must meet during a one-year period? For effective governance, a board generally needs to meet at least quarterly, preferably bimonthly and possibly monthly, but the bylaws should allow some leeway to the board. Who sets the schedule and place of board meetings?

Example: *The board of directors must meet at least quarterly and may hold its meetings at such times and places as a majority of the directors in office determine. The board may delegate this determination to the chair.*

2. Who may call a special meeting of the board—chair, executive director, and/or a certain number of directors? In some states, the members may call a meeting of the board.

Example: *Special meetings of the board of directors may be called at any time upon request of the chair, the executive director, or any two directors, provided that any such request shall specify the purpose of the meeting. Such a meeting shall be held with within fifteen days of such a request.*

3. What are the notification requirements regarding meetings? Bylaws generally indicate that written notice regarding the time and place of regular and special meetings must be sent to all board members a certain number of days prior to the meeting. A provision for waiving notice should be included, to allow directors to accept notice by telephone or other means.

Example: *Written notice of regular and special meetings shall be given not less than fifteen days prior to such meetings, provided, however, that any director may execute a written waiver of notice before or during the meeting, and the secretary shall enter it in the minutes or other records of the meeting.*

4. What is the quorum for a board meeting?

Example: *At all meetings of the board of directors, a majority of the directors then in office shall be necessary and sufficient to constitute a quorum for the transaction of business.*

5. Is a simple majority (the votes of half of the board members present plus one) sufficient to pass a motion at a meeting of the board? (Voting by proxy at a board meeting is illegal under the incorporation laws of most states.)

Example: *Except where otherwise required by law, the articles, or these bylaws, the affirmative vote of a majority of the directors present at a duly held meeting shall be sufficient for any action.*

6. Will "actions in writing" be authorized? An action in writing involves preparing a written motion or resolution and sending it to each director for his or her signature. This procedure makes it convenient to approve a required action against a deadline, especially when the action wouldn't generate much, if any, discussion.

Example: *Any action required or permitted to be taken at a meeting of the board of directors may be taken by a written action, provided that all of the directors approve the action. The written action is effective when signed by all directors, unless otherwise provided in the action.* (Most states require that actions in writing be unanimous and bear the signatures of all directors.)

7. What rules or procedures will be used to conduct meetings? Robert's Rules of Order are commonly used.

VI.   What shall be the duties of the OFFICERS?

1. What officers shall the corporation have? (Review the chapter on the board.) State law may require certain officers, but not all must be members of the board. How shall they be elected? (Some states provide that members may elect the officers.) How long may they serve?

Example: *The officers of the corporation shall be a chair* (or a president), *a vice chair* (or vice president), *a secretary, a treasurer, and such other officers as the board of directors may determine, and the officers shall be elected by affirmative vote of a majority of the board present at a duly held meeting. They shall serve terms fixed by the board of directors.*

2. How can officers be removed from their positions?

Example: *Any officer may be removed, with or without cause, by an affirmative vote of a majority of the directors present at a duly held meeting of the board of directors for which notice stating such purpose has been given in advance of the meeting.*

3. How can officers be replaced if they resign or are removed before the end of their terms?

Example: *A vacancy in an office because of death, resignation, or removal may be filled by the board of directors.*

4. What are the specific powers and duties of each officer?

Example: *The chair shall preside at all meetings of the board of directors and of the membership and shall oversee the long-term goals and strategies of the corporation. He or she shall serve as the liaison between the board and the* (title of the chief staff person, e.g., executive director or president) *and shall perform such other duties as determined by the board.*

The vice chair shall perform such duties as may be determined by the board of directors. The vice chair shall be vested with all powers of and perform all duties of the chair in the chair's absence or inability to act, but only so long as such absence or inability continues.

The executive director (or president) *shall be the chief executive officer of the corporation and shall be responsible for the day-to-day operations of the corporation. In addition, he or she shall perform such other duties as may be determined from time to time by the board of directors.*

The secretary shall attend all meetings of the board and any committees as directed thereof, and keep the minutes of such meetings, give notices, prepare any necessary certified copies of corpo-

rate records, and perform such other duties as may be determined from time to time by the board of directors.

The treasurer shall have charge of the corporate treasury, receiving and keeping the monies of the corporation and disbursing funds as authorized. The treasurer shall perform other such duties as may be determined by the board of directors.

5. Determine which officers are members of the board.

Example: *The chair and vice chair shall be members of the board of directors. All other officers may but need not be members of the board.*

VII. What will be the structure of the COMMITTEES?

See the chapter on the board. The bylaws may mention only that committees may be set up by the board and outline how they should work, may name specific committees and their functions, or may name only one or two committees and allow for the formation of others.

Alternative examples:

A. *The board of directors may establish one or more committees having the authority of the board in the management of the business of the corporation to the extent determined by the board. Committee members may be members of the board or other interested persons. The board may delegate the appointment of committees and their chairs to the board chair.*

B. *The board of directors will establish the following committees*: (see the chapter on the board for typical committees and their duties).

VIII. What SPECIAL RULES will apply to the corporation?

1. Will the corporation indemnify its board members (protect them from the financial consequences of liability lawsuits and judgments)? Your state may (as does Minnesota, for example) require indemnification unless the articles of incorporation or bylaws provide otherwise.

Example: *To the full extent permitted by the* (name of state) *Nonprofit Corporation Act, as amended from time to time, or by other provisions of law, each person who was or is a party or is threatened to be made a party to any threatened, pending, or completed action, suit, or proceeding, wherever and by whomsoever brought, including any such proceeding by or in the right of the corporation, whether civil, criminal, administrative, or investigative, by reason of the fact that he or she is or was a member, director, or officer of the corporation, shall be indemnified by the corporation by an affirmative vote of a majority of the directors present at a duly called meeting of the board of directors, against expenses, including attorneys' fees, judgments, fines, and amounts paid in settlement actually and reasonably incurred by such person in connection with such action. The indemnification shall inure to the benefit of the heirs, executors, and administrators of such person.*

2. What is the fiscal year of the corporation? This can be omitted from the bylaws and left to the board to determine.

IX. What are the provisions for AMENDMENT OF THE BYLAWS?

Example: *The board of directors may from time to time adopt, amend, or repeal all or any of the bylaws of this corporation.*

Legal Aspects: Cutting the Red Tape

There are a variety of legal matters that apply to nonprofit organizations, including registering with government agencies, filing reports, securing licenses, employment laws, and tax issues. Some of these concerns are governed by federal law; others, by state law. Some local governments may also have some requirements.

Most of the procedures for handling legal matters are fairly simple once you understand them. Although it is possible to go it on your own, it can be helpful, timesaving, and reassuring to have professional legal advice, and there are attorneys who specialize in this area of law. Because attorneys' fees can be formidable, check to see whether you can get donated or inexpensive legal services through a legal assistance program or through the contacts of a board member.

Incorporation

It isn't necessary to incorporate in order to function on a tax-exempt basis. Some groups may be able to operate as loosely knit unincorporated associations. For example, if an association solicits contributions, it might find an established, incorporated nonprofit sympathetic to its purpose that will act as a "fiscal agent" (although this is not as simple as it might seem, and can present potential fiduciary issues for the fiscal agent). Or a group might work with an existing organization in the same service area to develop and operate a specific type of program.

Incorporation is advisable, however, because it provides the significant advantages outlined below.

What Does Incorporation Mean?

A *corporation* is a legal entity with rights, privileges, and liabilities separate from those of the individuals who invest money in it, compose its membership, and run it.

Even though a large number of businesses are sole proprietorships or partnerships, those doing the greatest volume of business and owning the most capital are organized in the corporate form. Incorporation is also a major form of organization for nonbusiness groups formed for artistic, educational, social, or charitable purposes. Incorporated nonprofit organizations do not generally have stockholders as do business corporations, but they do have boards of directors and may have voting members who act like shareholders. In addition, in most states the state attorney general is legally deemed to be the public's representative for dealing with misconduct of charities.

Corporations are generally formed under the provisions of state law. Usually, there are separate state statutes that govern incorporation procedures and requirements for nonprofit groups (the statute may use the term *not-for-profit*), including philanthropic, religious, social service, welfare, educational, patriotic, cultural, artistic, and public interest organizations. Formation of a corporation under such statutes creates a new entity with the following special characteristics:

1. *Limited liability:* The most important advantage of incorporation is that the individuals who control the corporation are not responsible, except in unusual situations, for the legal and financial obligations of the organization. Corporations can incur debts as a result of purchases, salary expenses, building mortgages, and service contracts. They can have legal obligations resulting from contracts and from alleged negligence or misdeeds. These debts and obligations are in the name of the corporation rather than in the names of the individuals who are its members. This reduces the risk to the personal assets of individuals involved in group ventures.

   In order to ensure their limited liability, the officers and directors should (1) make it clear when they are conducting the agency's business that they are doing so on behalf of the corporation, (2) make sure that the agency's funds are kept separate from the funds of individuals, (3) hold regular board meetings to review and conduct corporate business, (4) follow all other corporate formalities, and (5) make a reasonable effort to secure sufficient funds for the corporation to meet its obligations.

2. *Continuity:* A corporation will continue to exist "in perpetuity" until legal dissolution, unless it is chartered for only a specified, limited period of time. Its legal existence is not dependent on the continued participation of individual members or directors.

3. *Uniform set of rules:* Because the operation of corporations is governed by a uniform, though flexible, set of rules under state law, those involved in corporations and those who deal with them know how they should operate and what should be expected of them. For example, it is relatively easy to prove that the officers of a corporation are, in fact, authorized to enter into a contract on behalf of the corporation. It would be much more difficult to prove that individuals acting on behalf of an unincorporated organization are authorized to enter into a contract for the organization. Because, as noted above, the corporate form provides continuity (that is, the people who control it may change, but the corporation continues), some businesses, funders, and banks may prefer to deal with incorporated nonprofit organizations.

4. *Tax exemption:* An important reason for incorporation is that it facilitates application for tax-exempt status under federal and state income tax laws. However, it is important to understand that there is a difference between being "nonprofit" and being "tax-exempt." There are many nonprofits that do not qualify for exemption from federal or state income taxes.

How Does an Organization Incorporate?

A nonprofit organization becomes a corporation by drafting a legal incorporation document, or articles of incorporation, and filing it with the state. It is advisable for an organization to have legal assistance in filing for incorporation, but it is not required. In many cases, an attorney may simply review the articles of incorporation after the organizers complete the form.

Check your state's law on the minimum number of persons needed to act as incorporators. In Minnesota, for instance, only one person of legal age (18 or older) is required to form a corporation.

In choosing a name for your corporation, check with the appropriate state office to make sure that the same or a similar name is not being used by another group within the state. In some circumstances, such as if the organization will operate across state lines, a nationwide search may be necessary.

The state agency that registers new corporations often can supply a form for your articles of incorporation, but it may be sufficient only for meeting the state's legal requirements and may not be adequate if you intend to seek 501(c)(3) status (secure a copy of IRS Publication 557).

The information that should be included in the articles of incorporation varies from state to state, but may include some or all of the following items:

1. Name of the corporation.
2. Purpose of the corporation. The IRS is likely to pay close attention to this statement because it limits your activities to those consistent with your purpose, and your specific purposes must comply with what is permitted for tax-exempt status.
3. A statement that the corporation does not afford "pecuniary gain," or profit, to its members or others.
4. The period of duration of corporate existence, which may be perpetual.
5. The location of the organization's registered office.
6. Name and address of each incorporator.
7. Number of directors constituting the *initial* board of directors, the name and address of each director, and the tenure in office of the first directors. (The number need not be equal to the number the founders believe will be eventually established in the bylaws and elected. Check your state law for any minimum age requirements for directors.)
8. The extent of personal liability, if any, of members for corporate obligations and the methods of enforcement and collection (there will be none, except in unusual circumstances).
9. Whether the corporation has capital stock (most nonprofit corporations do not have capital stock).
10. Provisions for the distribution of corporate assets and for dissolution.
11. Whether or not there will be a membership separate from the board of directors.

When they are complete, the articles of incorporation are submitted to the state agency that handles incorporations. In some states, this is the secretary of state. A "certificate of incorporation" or a "charter" will be issued; at that time, the corporation legally begins its existence. Your state may require annual registration to maintain active status.

After the organization's incorporation, the first meeting of the directors should be held. During the first meeting, the initial bylaws should be adopted if not already established (some states require that the incorporators adopt the bylaws). The bylaws are needed early in the process, because they spell out how the board functions, officers to be elected, and possibly other business that needs to be conducted. (Even if your state law does not require bylaws, it is highly advisable to establish some, to help avoid questions of who can do what and how.) Your state law may also require that your organization conduct itself in a certain manner and within certain structural limitations, such as having officers, periodic meetings, and maintaining financial records and minutes. For membership organizations, the law may set out additional or different requirements.

Tax Exemption

Tax exemption is more complicated than people often realize, involving various types of taxes and levels of government and affecting the numerous types of nonprofits differently. Also, organizations that qualify for exemption from paying federal income taxes on some or all of their income are not necessarily eligible to receive contributions that are tax deductible for the donors.

Nonprofits classified as 501(c)(3) (named for the section of the Internal Revenue Code that applies) must operate for one or more of these purposes: "religious, educational, charitable, scientific, literary, testing for public safety, fostering national or international amateur sports competition or preventing cruelty to children or animals." These are generally referred to as charitable nonprofits.

A nonprofit not qualifying for the charitable exemption may qualify for exemption as a "social welfare" organization under section 501(c)(4) of the Internal Revenue Code. The fundamental difference between the two exemptions is not found in the ultimate purpose of each, but rather in the kinds of activities in which they engage. For example, civic organizations usually are classified as 501(c)(4). Contributions to 501(c)(4) organizations generally may not be claimed as charitable contributions on donors' income tax returns.

A charitable organization—501(c)(3)—may also engage in *limited* lobbying, unless it is a private foundation. Consult a legal specialist on tax exemption to find out exactly how far your organization may go in lobbying before getting into trouble with the IRS.

Federal Tax Exemption

Applications for tax-exempt status should be made within twenty-seven months from the end of the month in which the organization was created, or incorporated. Generally, the IRS will treat the organization as if it were 501(c)(4) for the period prior to filing for tax-exempt status. You should contact your local IRS office and ask for form 1023, the application form used to file for 501(c)(3) tax-exempt status, and IRS Publication 557, which provides detailed instructions for determining eligibility.

In addition to filing form 1023 for tax-exempt status, every exempt organization is required to have an employer identification number, regardless of whether it has any employees. An employer identification number is the official identification code for an organization (similar to a social security number for an individual) that is used by the Internal Revenue Service for tax-related purposes. To ensure the quickest validation for tax-exempt status from the IRS, you should file form SS-4 to secure your employer identification number as soon as possible, even before you file form 1023. Both forms can be obtained from a local IRS office. Note carefully where each form is to be sent.

You can file the application yourself, but it is better to have the assistance of an attorney. Copies of your articles of incorporation and your bylaws, if any, must be included with the application. If your application is approved, the Internal Revenue Service will respond with a letter that states that your organization is tax exempt and cites the exact code under which it is classified. It can take up to a year for the IRS to respond to an application, but it usually takes three to four months. When you receive the IRS letter, keep it in a safe place, because foundations and corporate funders generally require a *photocopy* of it if you apply for a grant. Never let the original letter leave your office.

Within five and one-half months after the end of your organization's fiscal year, tax-exempt 501(c)(3) organizations must file form 990, the "return" for organizations exempt from income tax, with the Internal Revenue Service. Your state *may* also require this form, although if a state does require a copy, some waive the filing for nonprofits whose annual revenues are under a certain amount, such as $25,000. Form 990 requires an accounting of all income, expenses, assets, and liabilities of the organization.

State Income Tax Exemption

After receiving federal tax-exempt status, nonprofits should apply for exemption from state income taxes if they are based in states with income tax and that require separate filing (some states do not). The procedure for filing for state income tax exemption is generally routine, as states usually follow the rulings of the Internal Revenue Service. State tax exemptions are granted by state departments of revenue.

Once your organization has received tax-exempt status from the state department of revenue, contact with that office may continue annually or may shift to another state agency. Organizations filing income tax form 990 with the Internal Revenue Service should also file annually a copy of the 990 with the state department of revenue or the state attorney general's office, whichever is required in the particular state. This procedure is only routine; it is just another one of the compliance rulings your organization must follow according to the law.

For application forms and further information on state income tax exemption for nonprofits, contact your state department of revenue.

State Sales Tax Exemption

In most states, sales tax is levied on various items sold to the general public (in retail sales). However, *some* nonprofit corporations *may* be exempt from paying sales taxes on goods purchased for their use. (Don't count on it; sales tax exemptions are hard to secure in most states.)

For an eligible nonprofit organization to purchase goods without paying the sales tax, it must provide the seller with a tax-exemption number. You can apply for such a number, known as a *certificate of exempt status*, from the state department of revenue. (For example, to apply for sales tax-exempt status in Minnesota, an organization must file form ST-16 with the Minnesota Department of Revenue.)

Once your organization has received its sales tax-exempt number, it is your responsibility to present the number at the time of purchase to enjoy the privilege of sales tax exemption. To receive sales tax-exemption forms, instructions, and general information, contact the nearest office of your state department of revenue.

Utilities Tax Exemption

Some organizations that qualify for federal and state tax exemption do not have to pay taxes on telephone or other utility bills. Generally, this is limited to certain 501(c)(3) educational institutions. Contact your telephone, gas, and electric companies for more information.

State and Local Registration Requirements

State and local laws may also require other types of registration for nonprofit organizations. Currently, about half of the states require annual registration, and a dozen require one-time registration or registration when using professional fund raisers.

Generally, the state attorney general regulates nonprofit organizations. Cities may require permits for groups raising funds within their boundaries. Groups organizing as nonprofit corporations should check with the secretary of state, office of the attorney general (it may have a division devoted to charitable organizations), or department of revenue in their state to determine which regulations apply to them. For example, in the state of Minnesota, the following requirements apply.

Registration with State Attorney General

Minnesota law requires registration and reports from the following nonprofit organizations: (1) those soliciting $25,000 or more per year from "public" sources, including foundations and individuals other than members, and (2) those paying a professional fund raiser. These organizations must file a registration statement and a financial report with the charities section of the state attorney general's office.

Each year, registered organizations must file an annual report on a prescribed form and a 990 financial statement following the close of the organization's annual accounting period. If the organization fails to file an annual report and a financial statement on time, the registration statement will no longer be effective. Therefore, if problems arise that will delay the filing of an annual report or financial statement, the organization should notify the charities review section and request an extension. Forms for the registration statement, the annual report, and the financial statement are available from the charities section. This unit also licenses all professional fund raisers who are hired on a consulting basis by nonprofit organizations.

In addition to the filing requirements outlined above, organizations with total revenues exceeding $350,000 in a year must submit an audit statement signed by a certified public accountant with their annual reports.

Charities Review Organizations

In addition to the National Charities Review Board, some similar state organizations exist that serve as "better business bureaus" for charitable organizations. For example, the Minnesota Charities Review Council is a nongovernmental nonprofit group that investigates charities that have been questioned by Minnesota citizens. It does not review every nonprofit organization in the state, only those about which it receives complaints or questions.

In such cases, the Charities Review Council requests information, primarily financial, from the organization, the state, and the city (if registration is required by the municipality), and then it makes this information available to the public. The council has no formal authority, but its close working relationship with the charities section of the attorney general's office indirectly gives its reports considerable weight.

Public Solicitation Licenses

Some municipalities require any nonprofit organization that intends to solicit funds within their limits to file for a permit, or solicitation license. (Ordinances of this type do not apply to those organizations soliciting from their own members only.) Solicitation licenses generally must be acquired each year and require annual reports of income, expenses related to solicitations, and expenditures of the organization.

For example, in Minneapolis, any nonprofit organization soliciting ten or more sources in the city within a year (including corporations, foundations, or individuals) is required to file for a solicitation license, with an annual fee. But in St. Paul, only those organizations that seek donations from individuals on the street are required to obtain permits.

If you plan a large funding campaign aimed toward several sources within one municipality, you should check with the city clerk to see whether a solicitation license is required.

Mission, Vision, and Strategic Goals: Creating the Formula

"Cheshire-Puss," she began, "would you tell me, please, which way I ought to go from here?"

"That depends a good deal on where you want to get to," said the Cat.

"I don't care much where —" said Alice.

"Then it doesn't matter which way you go," said the Cat.

Without a well-thought-out plan, which includes a clear statement of mission for your organization, a vision of the kind of organization you want to become, and well-defined goals and objectives for your programs, you not only handicap yourself in getting from here to there, but none of the people important to you will have a clear picture of where "there" is. Good planning involves both a long-range view—generally called a *strategic plan*—and a set of short-term objectives and related activities to undertake—sometimes called the *annual plan*, *tactical plan*, or *operating plan*.

For both long-range and short-term plans, typically there are three ways you might go about planning. The first way is all in your head. You've already spent much time thinking about the needs your program will address and how you want to do that, or you wouldn't be starting up a new nonprofit organization. Maybe you're one of those people who can have all that so well organized in your head that you can talk easily about the mission, vision, and strategies to potential members of the board, funders, and other constituencies.

The second way to plan is to put ideas down on paper, an exercise that can help focus your own thinking and help the people important to your future success understand just what, why, how, when, and where you'll do what you intend to do. Satisfied that you've completed some sacred rite, you then tuck the plan away somewhere and go on with your work.

The third way of planning is to take the written ideas, approved by your board, and keep them *continually* in front of everyone who has a role to play in making your organization a success. The ideas and goals you've written down drive your annual plans, priorities, and other critical decisions. You share them with potential funders, staff, and volunteers. You sit down with staff and board periodically and see if they still make sense. This third way of planning is what this chapter is all about.

Strategic Planning

There are about as many ways to develop and write a strategic plan as there are books, seminars, and consultants dealing with the subject (and there are a lot of each). However, there are some generally accepted guidelines:

1. A good strategic plan should work for your organization for three to five years. However, periodically you should consider whether revisions are needed, especially throughout your organization's early stages, when assumptions may fall apart or new opportunities may develop; when you conclude that services should be modified or new ones added; when external threats loom; and every year even when everything seems to be going well.

2. Planning is an important management activity. It focuses the staff's activities around goals and objectives that reflect a defined set of organizational values, resource capacity, and future opportunities.

3. Planning is usually initiated by the leadership—the executive director or the board of directors—but the more people involved and the more information gathered, the better the plan is likely to be and the better it will drive important decisions and activities.

4. On the other hand, the longer the planning process takes, the less current will be the plan, the more weary people will grow of the effort, and the more likely the planning process will fizzle out before a good plan is completed.

5. A strategic plan should start with a statement of the organization's *mission*—what does it exist to do? It should include a *vision*—what kind of organization are you going to become?

The plan should include an honest analysis of the needs your programs will serve, how you'll serve them, specific goals, resources required, strengths, weaknesses, opportunities, and threats.

6. The strategic plan should drive the annual plan — the specific activities that support your organization's mission and will lead you to achieve your vision.

A Step-by-Step Process

Step 1: Create a Planning Group

It's tempting to do all the planning yourself — it's certainly more efficient, and you don't have to argue with people who don't see things your way. However, doing it by yourself is pretty risky. You can get far down the road with your plan only to discover that there is a point of view, some knowledge, some experience, some expectation, that you should have considered back at the beginning. Although your actual planning group doesn't have to involve everyone with something to contribute to the plan, it should consist of the key people who will help you put the organization and its programs together. For example, a planning group for a new, small nonprofit might consist of the chief executive, one or more other staff members if any, the chair of the board, someone from the board or a key volunteer who knows something about planning, and someone who can see things from the perspective of potential clients.

Step 2: Create a Mission Statement

The mission statement describes the purpose of the organization — the essence of why it exists. It generally identifies its target audience and may refer to its geographic area of operation. The staff, board, volunteers, and clientele will best believe in the mission if they participate in its development. The statement should be short enough that staff, board, and volunteers can recite it from memory. For example: *The Self Sufficiency Center motivates and assists low-income people in the metropolitan area to develop and implement individualized, realistic self-sufficiency action plans.*

Step 3: Establish Your Vision Statement

The vision statement sets forth the expected future of the organization. All of your constituencies should understand what is expected over the long term so that everyone can focus on that desired outcome. Again, you should keep the vision statement as short as possible. For example: *The Arts Center will become the city residents' first place of choice for studying, experiencing, and supporting the humanities.*

Step 4: State Your Guiding Values

Stating your organization's values or guiding principles (and insisting that everyone live up to them) is important. These principles spell out the ethical framework of how things get done. They tell all of your stakeholders what kind of organization you are. Some examples:

- *The Center believes that all people, regardless of social or economic condition, have the capacity to take charge of their lives and should be enabled and empowered to make critical decisions for their futures.*
- *We value the full range of human diversity and seek to involve diverse populations in our staff, board, volunteers, and clientele.*
- *We ask and listen to our clients describe the services they need and the way they want them delivered.*
- *We will never do anything that would embarrass us if printed in tomorrow's newspaper.*

Step 5: Define the Problem or the Need

You've already defined an existing problem or need to some extent, or you wouldn't have this wonderful concept for a new nonprofit organization. But do you have all the information you'll need to demonstrate to funders and anyone else important to you that this is something worth tackling?

Identify the specific concerns and define the target audience on which your organization will focus. Invite people from your potential client group to help you. Gather data to substantiate any theories and personal experiences of those doing the planning. Talk to people with professional, governmental, or other expertise in your intended service area. Survey the related literature in professional and general-interest journals and any local reports or studies on the topic. Talk to people operating similar existing programs. In short, involve all of your stakeholders in this process.

The results of your needs assessment may or may not totally support your original assumptions. For example, you may discover that what creates the needs or problems you intend to address is not what you originally thought.

From the initial list of problems, you may decide to select one or two that your program realistically can work on in its first years, given practical limitations of resources. On what situations can you have a significant impact? (There may be some aspects of a problem over which you can have no control or influence.) Be specific in selecting and defining your target client population. For instance, a program should be designed not for "youths," but for a specific group of youth, such as youths aged 12 to 18 in a specific neighborhood who are identified as using drugs extensively. The better you are able to define the target audience, the more likely it is your program will be effective in meeting the needs of its clients.

As a result of the needs assessment process, you should develop a statement of the problem and the defined client population. For example:

- Needs statement: *Working mothers critically need a readily accessible, reliable, and affordable service to refer them to quality child-care providers who meet the mothers' varying requirements.*
- Problem statement: *Many elderly citizens in the community are forced to give up living independently because they lack transportation, are unable to perform heavy housekeeping and maintenance tasks, and no longer have regular personal or family contacts.*
- Client population: *Residents in the downtown neighborhood over age 65 who live independently but who need assistance to continue living in their own homes or apartments.*

Step 6: Lay Out Your Goals

Goals define the intended outcomes of what you intend to do. They are concise statements of what a program is designed to accomplish. They are the long-term aims of the organization and are driven by the organization's mission and vision.

A goal can be stated in the form of a description of a new condition that the program will achieve through the services provided. A goal statement would not necessarily describe your year-to-year objectives or program activities, but would set forth what will result from them. It should be stated in terms of some measurable criteria. For example: *Successfully assist single parents to secure jobs that produce economic benefits greater than dependency on welfare programs.*

A goal may or may not have an ending point. For instance, it's likely there will always be new single parents who need help to become self-sufficient; on the other hand, eradicating smallpox was a goal that was fully completed.

The achievement of goals requires good strategies (described shortly) and specific, short-term objectives (defined in the section on the annual plan). Although goals and objectives can form a sturdy framework for program planners, many planners choose not to differentiate between the two. Instead, they describe their program plans in a series of goal/objective statements that may be either short or long term. You must decide which format works best for you.

Be sure that your goal/objective statements describe measurable outcomes. These outcome statements should refer specifically to who will be affected; describe what these people are expected to do, under what conditions, and how well or to what extent; and include a time factor.

Goals need to be written clearly and simply, in terms free of jargon and ambiguity that can be easily understood by anyone, within or outside the organization.

Step 7: Assess Present Organizational Conditions

Your next step is to analyze the present conditions related to your organization. Determine your organization's capacity for having a meaningful impact on the defined problem and identify any factors that may limit that capacity. You may want to subdivide this assessment into an analysis of assumptions, strengths, weaknesses, opportunities, and threats.

Regardless of how you organize this part of the strategic plan, you need to set forth how doable it will be for your organization to bring about a favorable change in the problem defined. What are the factors in your favor? These could include available financial and human resources, community support, legislative concerns, support of key people, existing programs related to the problem, and favorable attitudes among your constituency.

Often it's helpful to include the assumptions that are driving the design of your organization and its program. What are the premises about human behavior, the attitudes, and the principles that will form the basis of the program? Although in many groups and programs these assumptions are unspoken, they are always present, directly influencing program format and outcome. Just as the problem-related data provide the *objective* answer to the question "Why this program?" these assumptions and value statements are your *subjective* response to the question. If you are conscious of these assumptions, you can use them positively to develop your program and you can eliminate assumptions that may not be valid or those upon which the planning group does not agree. Discuss and identify your assumptions and values as a group. Although there may not be total agreement, the planning group should be able to reach a consensus about the underlying assumptions of the program you propose. For example: *Children benefit educationally and emotionally from contact with the arts.*

Don't overlook identifying any forces that could drive the continuation of the defined problem or limit your impact. These could include lack of financial and community support, negative factors in the community or population that are difficult or impossible to control, and lack of support of key people. Some factors can be addressed by your program. Are there facilitating factors that could be implemented to counteract the negative factors or threats?

Step 8: Develop the Strategies

You have finally reached the stage at which you are ready to plan the strategies needed to accomplish your goals, such as the services your program will offer and how they will be provided. This includes determining which strategies will best eliminate or weaken the factors that limit your efforts, strengthen the facilitating factors, and promote the achievement of your goals.

A first step is to brainstorm with your staff, volunteers, and board about all of the possible strategies that relate to your goals. What approaches to this problem have been tried in the past? With what results? Are any particular strategies suggested by pertinent research or literature? Are there any similar programs in your community or in other areas on which you want to model your program? If other projects addressing this problem have not been successful, how will your program be different? What approach is most feasible, in terms of your resources, values, and goals? Which strategies will overcome the limiting factors and strengthen the facilitating factors you have identified previously? Which methods are most likely to be supported by funding sources? Which would be most acceptable to your target population or constituency? Are there other organizations already involved with the need you've defined with which you should partner in some way?

From these possibilities, your planning group must select an approach to the problem that is feasible, consistent with your values and beliefs, appropriate for your constituencies, and likely to achieve the desired outcome. For example:

- *Maximize our resources and the impact on our clientele by developing a collaboration with another nonprofit that is providing human services to our target population.*
- *Involve all staff, board, and representatives of our clients to develop a diversity initiative that will address our identified diversity issues and opportunities and increase our total organizational effectiveness.*

The Annual (Tactical) Plan

The major elements of the annual or tactical plan include *objectives*, *actions* (together with who is responsible for taking those actions and a timeline), and a *budget*.

Step-by-Step Process

Step 1: Establish Your Objectives

What you, your staff, and/or your volunteers must do to achieve your goals should include specific steps with stated points in time for completion, six months out or twelve months. Objectives are more specific than goals and break down broad goals into smaller components that describe more narrowly defined achievements. Like goals, objectives focus on results rather than on methods. Like goals, objectives should be feasible, measurable, and stated so that they are clearly understandable to anyone.

The plan should contain exact measurement references related to anticipated achievement levels of each objective. Often, precise estimates regarding performance will be projected. It is important that these projected "success" rates be realistic and, if possible, that they be based on the experiences of similar programs.

Objectives should be specific. For each objective, or projected outcome, ask yourself *who* will be affected, *what* is going to occur, *when*, *how*, and *what* will be the indicator of desired outcome? For example: *Assist low-income, single mothers to identify five to eight community resources or agencies available to help them secure child care, health services, family planning, income maintenance, vocational training, and counseling.* (Such an objective likely would be only one among several steps taken to help low-income, single mothers achieve more self-sufficiency.)

Note that this objective is measurable. Whatever approaches are used, how many mothers were assisted as described, and so on, can be determined. Too often, objectives mean little because they are not specific enough to be measurable and don't include specific measures of outcomes. If you cannot measure how well you have achieved something, neither you nor your constituencies can be sure you have accomplished anything. The standard of measurement specified in an objective may be results of pretests and posttests or questionnaires, observable behavior (pregnancy, court adjudication, legislation passed), or simply the number of people completing a program successfully.

Whenever the performance stated in an objective is abstract or covert (e.g., putting training to work, change of attitudes, or renewed commitment to something), you should add an overt behavior to the objective (measurable or observable) that might indicate whether the covert performance has been achieved. For example: *Eighty percent of the single mothers participating in the program will develop specific actions they will agree to undertake in the following six months.*

Not all objectives in the annual plan are necessarily related to programs, of course. For instance, you may have an objective for securing a certain level of funding and an objective for operating within your approved budget.

Step 2: Develop the Actions (Activities) and Timetable to Achieve the Objectives

Plans for how to achieve objectives should be stated in terms of specific actions to be taken: set up a certain number of workshops, provide counseling to a given number of clients, deliver a certain number of meals to the homebound, teach parenting skills, sponsor cultural events, lobby for environmental causes. Describe these activities as specifically as possible. Each activity should be matched to the objective that it supports. (An activity can relate to more than one objective, and vice versa.)

Each activity should be put into a time frame. When will it start? How long will it take? How often will it be done? When will it be completed? Assign primary responsibility for each activity and task within an activity to a specific person, and also note who else will contribute to it. An activity calendar can then be formulated that will summarize the work plan for the organization.

Step 3: Prepare a Budget

Budgeting for the organization is covered in the chapter titled "Managing Financial Outcomes: Budgeting the $$$$." Generally, the overall budget is developed from the bottom up; that is, you consider everything you want to do in the coming year, figure out what that will cost, add that figure to fixed annual costs, such as rent and utilities, and there's your budget. However, unless you can always secure the resources required to do everything you want to do, that "first cut" of a budget probably has to be revised from the top down, but working with your staff on sorting out the essentials and top priorities.

In summary, the written annual plan will include the following items:

1. A set of objectives
2. The actions that will be taken to achieve the objectives, deadlines, who has overall responsibility for each action, and who else must be involved
3. A calendar of the detailed tasks required to complete the actions
4. A list of task assignments
5. The organization's budget

Your First Annual Plan

Your first annual plan will be especially challenging and critical. This plan is likely to determine the skills and size of the staff and/or volunteers you need to provide your services and achieve your objectives. It may also determine what size and structure is necessary for your office space, equipment, and so on.

Evaluating Your Organization's Effectiveness

As noted earlier in this chapter, an evaluation system is the means by which an organization determines the impact of its programs on the areas on which it focuses. It is important for evaluation purposes that goals and objectives are measurable. If your program is doing things that cannot be evaluated or measured, you may be unable to demonstrate that you are achieving anything.

Choose the criteria by which you will judge whether your goals and objectives have been achieved. There are several common ways to measure outcomes, including the following:

1. Counting the number of people served. (This may work fairly well for a museum, theater, community center, transportation service, and other programs where it can be reasonably assumed that a program is achieving a useful purpose if a certain number of people voluntarily use it. It doesn't do much, if anything, for determining the *effectiveness* of a social services program.)
2. Using appropriate tests or questionnaires at the point of intake (the point at which clients enter your service process) and program completion to measure changes in attitudes, well-being, and/or knowledge.
3. Comparing reported behavior before and after program involvement (through health records, court records, self-reporting, or reporting by professionals or other family members).
4. Surveying participants (and their families and/or concerned professionals—teachers, counselors, and so on) to determine satisfaction with the program.
5. Comparing those served with others from the target population who did not receive your services (interesting to do, but usually very difficult).

Choose methods appropriate for each objective. Use more than one means of measurement when possible and affordable.

Develop Means of Recording Observable Changes

The means used to record observable changes are related directly to the measurement methods chosen and can include designing forms, developing surveys and questionnaires, and choosing appropriate tests. These can be developed by the staff alone or with the aid of outside consultants.

Decide on a Reporting System

The data gathered from the various records kept by the organization should form the basis of quarterly and annual reports. The reports should relate directly to the goals and objectives in your program plan, and they should provide a means for comparing achievements to planned performance. Your board, volunteers, and funders will be interested in these reports.

Decide who will be responsible for designing forms, maintaining records, and reporting. You may wish to consider getting the assistance of an outside consultant during any or all of these stages. Remember to include any proposed consultant fees in the program budget. The program plan, then, also serves as an evaluation tool. It tells you where you are going, how you will get there, and how you will know when you have arrived.

Implementing and Monitoring the Work Plan

Two different common and critical mistakes are often made after a work plan is developed. Either the plan is filed in the back of a dusty, unused drawer and ignored until close to year end, when someone remembers you probably should report something to the board, or the plan is followed slavishly, so that new developments or other indications of the need to change priorities or other elements of the plan are ignored.

After being sure that everyone who has a piece of the plan to handle clearly understands his or her responsibilities, you should monitor progress by periodically (monthly or quarterly) reviewing "where you're at" in terms of your original plan. You're a good manager if you alter an objective or activity because of more important new issues or developments, but be sure revision is necessary and not just an alibi for poor performance. Set up the new objectives, activities, or whatever just as you did the other ones.

Reviewing the Program Plan and Repeating the Planning Process

Planning should be a continual cycle of monitoring, analyzing, thinking, planning, evaluating, monitoring, analyzing, and so on. After the first year of operating under a thorough, written plan, sit down with the staff and your board and review what worked well and what didn't. Were the objectives realistic? Too many or too few? Did you achieve what you wanted? Why not? Should any changes be made in the planning process itself? Did you involve everyone who could contribute something of value?

In practice, this planning process is not as rigid as it appears on paper. Your planning group should examine this model and consider how it can best be applied to your organization. In some cases, it will be frustrating to try to quantify the objectives of your program. Some of your program's accomplishments may not be objectively measured. Nevertheless, it is important to try to measure, as specifically as possible, the outcomes of your program. A well-designed program plan gives an organization a clear destination and a way to tell whether or not it got there. One aspect of this process should be considered rigid: involve your clients at every step.

Managing Financial Outcomes: Budgeting the $$$$

The budget is the financial blueprint of your organization. It is the plan that sets out your desired financial outcomes — what you intend to accomplish financially during a specific period, usually a year. (The annual twelve-month period used for financial planning purposes is called a *fiscal year*. Often, this corresponds to the calendar year — January through December — but your fiscal year can begin with any month.)

The budget should clearly establish what should happen in *both* revenues and expenditures as a result of your service programs, fund raising, and so on. Don't just outline what you want to spend and assume the money to cover expenses will be found somewhere as the year progresses. Realistically budget the expected sources of income — grants, government contracts, members' contributions, fees, and donations of services and supplies. New organizations should be conservative in forecasting income, which means, of course, being conservative in estimating what you can afford to spend.

How Is a Budget Used?

A budget should be used for financial planning and cash management throughout the year. Plan on reviewing your budget at least quarterly, and perhaps monthly. Regular budget reviews should determine whether actual income and expenses have deviated from the budget *and why*. Differences between actual and budgeted income and expenses may result from seasonal expenses, unanticipated expenses, delayed funding, insufficient fund raising efforts, or an unrealistic budget. When discrepancies arise, the financial plan must be revised to reflect the real situation. If your original estimates for expenses and/or income are not realistic, adjust them during regular budget reviews. If the budget review indicates an upcoming crunch or deficit, you must take corrective action to avoid a financial crisis. Such action may include expanding your fund raising and/or cutting back on expenses. The earlier corrective action is taken, the more likely it is that you will be able to avoid cutting back on staff and programs or going into debt. Effective use of the budgeting process allows you to catch small problems and alleviate them before the organization finds itself in a financial stranglehold.

Another budget area of immediate usefulness is that of fund raising. You need to know how much money you must raise to conduct your anticipated programs for at least a one-year period. A carefully constructed budget is essential to your funding proposal. The budget is an indication to funders of your planning and management skills. The funds your program requires must be projected clearly so that the organization's needs can be understood and accepted by potential funders.

However, don't make the mistake of hanging your budget on at the end of your grant proposal and forgetting it! Your budget should be used as an ongoing management tool by the staff and board of directors. If you shelve it until the end of your fiscal year, you may well find that you are having difficulty making ends meet long before your next fiscal year ends. Engage, *with your staff*, in "contingency planning." That is, think through what you will do if revenues do not develop month to month as you have planned or if some unusual expense occurs. (It's best that the original budget be developed with the participation of all key staff people. Such participation can gain for the organization a broader perspective, greater knowledge, and stronger staff commitment.)

How Do You Develop a Budget?

The starting point of any budget is your strategic plan, as well as the annual plans you have developed to achieve your strategic plan, because those plans should have led to well-planned programs or projects for which funding can be secured. When you have determined in detail your goals and objectives, outlined your programs, considered funding sources, and planned your staffing pattern, you are ready to develop the budget.

What kind of a staff do you need, and what should you pay them? (New organizations may be doing well to afford one staff person; some may operate with only one part-time employee.) What are your space and equipment needs and what will these cost? (A new organization may initially operate out of a founder's house or from a desk in the office of another, friendly nonprofit.) What about conferences, publications, and other items you feel are necessary to keep the staff informed? How much will it cost to inform the public of your program (to pay for printing, mass mailings, posters, and the like)?

Fledgling organizations will find it more difficult to project future expenses without the financial records and past experience that older agencies use as a basis for future budgeting. It is helpful to discuss expenses with, and review the budgets of, managers of other programs similar to yours.

The budget is usually developed by the agency's executive director, but the first year the board probably will be involved from the beginning. Regardless of who prepares the budget, it is important that the skills and experience of other staff people and the board members be used throughout the process of budget development. Final approval of the budget is the responsibility of the board of directors as a whole. Development of the budget usually should begin three to six months before the onset of the new fiscal year and be approved by the beginning of the new year.

What Should a Budget Include?

The budget should include all of the anticipated income and expenditures of an organization during a fiscal year. The income includes *earned revenues*, for which a service must be performed, such as ticket sales and fees for services, and *contributed revenues*, grants and individuals' contributions, including equipment, other goods, and services that are donated. The expenditures include all of the costs of purchasing the services, space, and supplies necessary to operate your program. The fiscal year is a 365-day financial record-keeping period beginning on the date designated by the board of directors (or as stated in the organization's bylaws).

A budget includes both fixed and variable costs. *Fixed costs* are those that occur regardless of the level of activity or service. Examples are most salaries, insurance, and rent. *Variable costs* change directly with the level of use or activity. Postage, printing, and publication costs are usually variable. Telephone expenses are both fixed and variable—there are monthly phone service charges, which are fixed unless you eliminate some phone lines, and charges for long-distance calls, which vary.

Fixed costs are easier to determine than variable costs, although you should take into account any anticipated changes during the year, such as rent increases and salary increases. You must estimate variable costs as best you can, but you should remember to include seasonal as well as average monthly costs. For instance, postage estimates should include the cost of postage used each month as well as the annual bulk mail permit fee and the cost of the several bulk mailings you may have planned for the coming year.

Be realistic! New nonprofits usually start out with modest budgets and equally modest expectations of funding. Some will begin life operating out of someone's home or using a desk at another agency's office.

How Do You Determine Annual Expense Items?

Human Resources

Salaries: The salaries for each regular, paid staff position, whether full-time or part-time, should be determined separately to develop a total budget for employees. These salary figures should reflect employee income before state and federal taxes are withheld. You can develop salary schedules for various positions by calling similar organizations within your community and requesting information on their salary schedules. Salary determination should be based on what you need to pay to attract people with the skills you need to perform your services. (See also the information on employment laws in the chapter on human resources.)

Temporary Employees: The amount of money needed to pay temporary people used periodically is more difficult to determine than the amount needed for salaried workers. You must consider the types of tasks to be performed, the amount of time it will take to perform them, and the hourly wages for each type of job. If you will use an agency that provides temporary workers, its fee will include wages, FICA, and so on. Again, the amount needed for each job should be calculated separately to arrive at a total budget item for temporary workers.

Consultants: Consulting fees cover payments to people who provide services directly to the staff, such as trainers, accountants, and evaluators. Fees for an annual financial audit can be included here. (An audit may not be legally required, but funders may require it; fees for an audit can be substantial unless you arrange for the service to be contributed in whole or in part.)

FICA: Call your local Social Security Administration office to get the current FICA/Medicare rate.

Health and Life Insurance: Although currently legally optional, health and life insurance are benefits provided by most employers to their full-time staff (and often to part-time staff working a certain number of hours weekly). New nonprofits, of course, may decide they must defer offering these benefits until they're better established. Insurance costs depend on the type and amount of coverage purchased and the ages of the individuals covered (some state laws may restrict differences in rates on the basis of age). Call a couple of insurance agents and ask them for quotes on both health and life insurance (a board member may be able to refer you to reliable agents). Ask similar organizations about their insurance programs and rates. It's best to have a firm quote before you finalize your budget.

Retirement Plan: New, small nonprofits may not immediately establish retirement plans. Some never do. Eventually, you'll find it difficult to retain experienced, talented people without some sort of retirement plan. This could take the form of the organization's contributing an amount equal to a set percentage of an employee's salary to a plan, with the employee responsible for deciding how to invest the funds. This places the fiduciary responsibility for the ultimate outcome on the employee and not the employer. Get some professional advice before proceeding with any kind of retirement plan.

Unemployment Insurance: A tax may be required of all organizations and businesses within your state to maintain a public state fund for unemployment benefits, or it may apply only to organizations with more than a certain number of employees. Such benefits are based on a percentage of an employee's wages. Call the taxation division in your state to determine the rate of taxation for your organization.

Social Security: Social security (FICA/Medicare) taxes that must be deducted from the wages of employees must be determined, because an equal contribution is made by the employer.

Staff Development: An organization should try to make some funds available to be used by employees for further education and training in their fields, including management development for managers.

Physical Facility

Rent: If you will rent space and have not arranged for it at the time you develop your budget, it will be hard to determine an exact rental figure. You should identify a potential area for your office and ask a real estate agent for the going rate, per square foot, for office space in that area. After you have determined the amount of space needed in terms of square feet, multiply this figure by the rate estimate. (Be sure to ask what is included in the estimate — any parking, custodial care, light, heat, storage, and so on.)

If you plan to share a facility with an existing agency, determine the amount of space you will occupy and multiply this by the rate per square foot the agency is paying.

Utilities: Monthly charges for heat, electricity, and water may or may not be included in rent payments. If most of your rent estimates include utilities, you do not need a separate budget item for them. However, if they do not, ask potential landlords for estimates of monthly utilities payments.

Telephone: Ask the local phone company for a rate schedule. Rates will vary depending upon the type of system chosen and the number of phones installed. Don't forget to get a quote on the cost of installation and add it to your first year's budget. Also, estimate the cost of anticipated long-distance calls. Consider the value of voice mail service.

Janitorial Services: Rental or lease agreements may not include cleaning services for your office space, trash service, or pickup of recycled materials. Estimates for janitorial services are based on the square footage of your office space. Include this item in your budget if your rent estimates do not include janitorial services.

Purchased Equipment: First, list the items needed: desks, chairs, tables, file cabinets, personal computers, computer software, fax machine, copier, calculators, and so on. If you are just starting out, these costs can be very high. At least initially, you may need to seek alternatives to purchasing new equipment, such as buying used or rebuilt equipment and soliciting donations from corporations of furniture and equipment (call a corporation and ask for the person in charge of contribution giving; even if that corporation doesn't donate equipment, this person may be able to refer you to other sources).

Today's world of personal computers provides major clerical productivity and other advantages. New organizations often start with personal computers and printers donated by for-profit companies. This may be necessary, but it is not ideal, because your employees may wind up with computers that can't share data or diskettes or that don't run the software you need. If possible, determine the kind of software you need before you decide on the hardware.

Finally, try to include an item in the budget for depreciation of equipment; that is, set money aside for the inevitable time when you will need to replace worn-out or obsolete equipment. (However, a new organization may not be able to set up a depreciation account in its early years.) Established nonprofits generally have a "capital budget" that includes the purchase of equipment that has a useful life of longer than a year.

Leased Equipment: Instead of purchasing equipment such as fax and copying machines, you can rent it on a monthly basis or on longer leases. Call various rental businesses and seek quotes on the items you need. Sometimes rental payments can be applied to the possible subsequent purchase price of the equipment.

Equipment Maintenance: Machines such as copiers require regular maintenance, especially as they get older. If you own such equipment, ask an office equipment dealer about the cost of maintenance contracts. Often a copier can be leased, with maintenance included.

Other Costs

Insurance: Your organization will likely need several kinds of insurance: bonding, theft, fire, vehicle, workers' compensation, general liability, and directors and officers (D&O) liability. Talk to an insurance agent about your needs and the costs of each type of insurance your organization requires. States generally require businesses and organizations to provide for compensation to employees for salary lost and expenses incurred from injuries or diseases caused by work-related tasks. The purchase of a workers' compensation insurance policy is usually mandated. Call the workers' compensation division of your state's department of labor for information on the regulations and rates that apply to your organization. The rates are related to the risk of injury that each job entails—for instance, an office worker has a lower risk of injury than does a construction worker. It is important that you understand workers' comp classifications. Talk to your insurance agent before you classify your employees.

Loan Repayments: If you've taken out a loan, obviously you must budget for regular installment payments.

Supplies: This is tough to budget! It is hard to figure how many pencils, pens, paper, envelopes, letterhead, staples, tape, and so on a specific number of staff members will go through in one year. Check with organizations that are of similar size with similar functions to see how much they spend. An alternative is to make a list of the items you think will be needed and visit an office supply store to check prices.

Postage: There is no way to calculate the actual number of letters you plan to write per year, so just make a stab at it and multiply that number by the going postal rate. If you plan mailings of more than two hundred letters, flyers, or newsletters at a time, check into the cost of a bulk mail permit. For such bulk mailings, estimate the number and size of the mailings you might do in a year and check with the post office for the going rate per piece for bulk mail permit holders (it is much lower than other rates). There is an annual bulk mail permit fee, so be sure to include that fee in your budget also if you elect to get such a permit.

Books/Subscriptions: First, identify the newsletters and magazines you want and obtain subscription costs for each. Next, make a list of the books and other written materials (training manuals, directories) you know you should have, with their prices. Leave some room in the budget for other materials of which you may not yet be aware. If your organization is new and you are planning to develop a library of materials, plan to spread the cost of these materials over two or three years. This can be an expensive endeavor, especially if you try to do it in one chunk. Books on nonprofit management may be available at your local public or college library.

Services Purchased: Services you should consider in developing your budget may include payroll, bookkeeping, and computer time, as well as other service contracts.

Printing: This is another difficult item to estimate. Try to make an educated guess about monthly photocopying needs (for smaller copying jobs) and printing needs (for larger copying jobs). Commercial copy centers have price lists available, and, again, it may be helpful to talk to someone in a similar organization. Watch your costs closely during the first few months of the budget year; you may need to revise this budget item during the year.

Conferences: This may be a low priority, especially in the organization's initial years, but attending conferences and workshops can keep your staff informed about their fields, can trigger ideas, and can help to motivate workers and management.

Travel: Usually the biggest single item in the travel budget comprises mileage reimbursement and parking fees for employees' use of their personal cars for organization business. Calculate the number of miles per month each staff person may need to drive for job-related purposes. Estimate yearly costs on the basis of these figures by using a set per mile reimbursement figure, obtained by calling other nonprofits to determine the usual local rate.

Advertising: This includes newspaper advertising for staff positions as well as any advertising of your program in the community. There are many low-cost ways to advertise your program, so you need not plan on an expensive media campaign before you try other approaches (see the chapter on community relations).

Fees: Itemize any fees for memberships and licenses you anticipate for staff members and for the organization and fees charged by your bank on the organization's checking account.

Petty Cash: This is a cash fund used for small office expenses. It shouldn't be an actual budget category; rather, set it up for an amount that is replenished monthly, require receipts for all disbursements, keep close track of the expenses, and include them in the appropriate expense categories (such as supplies and postage).

How to Determine the Income Budget

The second part of the budget outlines planned income. An agency rarely has a total commitment for funding for an upcoming year at the time it begins the budgeting process. Therefore, it is necessary that you estimate as accurately as possible the income from those recurring sources upon which you depend for funds.

Most nonprofits need to obtain a significant percentage of their revenues from fees or other "earned income" in order to survive. Arts groups sell tickets to performances or exhibits. Human service agencies charge fees for services (to those served, to a government agency contracting with the nonprofit to provide services, or to some other third party, such as an insurer). Educational organizations charge fees for courses.

If you intend to provide some services for fees, you should begin by determining an appropriate fee structure. What direct and overhead costs must be covered? (Direct costs are those necessary to provide the service itself; overhead costs include a fair share of rent, supplies, phone, and so on.) Will you have a sliding fee schedule (some clients pay the full cost and others don't, based on their income)? What do other providers of similar services charge? Can you test your fee schedule by talking to likely users? Then, estimate how many participants you will serve in each of your programs during the coming year.

Contributions from individuals may also play an important part in your income plan. Funds to be raised from any special events and benefits can and should be estimated (remember to include a realistic budget for putting on such events). Another source of income could be earnings on endowment investments, if you have any.

Because the above-mentioned sources of funds are more in your control than are grants, you must try to be as precise as possible in estimating the income you expect to derive from these. The balance of your support, depending upon your specific programs, will come from various private or public grants.

Outline as precisely as possible all the grants you anticipate receiving from outside sources. Be reasonable in your expectations, taking into account any past experience with the funders and/or your initial inquiries. This step of budget development is especially difficult for new programs, which have no funding history on which to base projections. At this stage, you should ask those sources you are most sure of to confirm their interest in you and to estimate the amounts of their grants.

When the anticipated income from all these sources is added together, the difference between this figure and your expense budget is the amount you still need to raise from undetermined sources. Mostly these will be foundations and corporations you have not previously approached or of whom you are less sure. If this figure is a large portion of your budget, you may have set unrealistically high income goals for yourself, and you should consider either trimming back expenses or rethinking what you can achieve from other sources of income. Calling on potential funders to share your vision and financial needs before you make a formal request could help you estimate the likelihood of meeting your grants income objective.

When you present your proposed budget to your board, you should be prepared to outline prioritized spending decreases or increases from initial budget plans, depending upon the progress you make with your funding sources.

What Budget Format Should Be Used?

A budget usually is set up in one of three formats. The first, and simplest, merely lists revenues and expenses according to the categories set out in the previous chapter sections (this is called a *summary budget*.) This format is used for the budgets of organizations that are small and/or that have fairly simple organizational and programming structures.

The second format outlines the organization's expenses according to the service or program areas (this is called a *functional budget*). For instance, a community clinic that provides an extensive counseling program and an educational outreach program as well as clinical services may find it most useful to organize its budget in terms of those program areas. This format outlines the costs of providing each of these services. Often, organizations raise funds separately for each program area, and the functional budget format is essential in those cases.

A functional budget may or may not have a separate column for overall administrative costs. These are expenses that relate directly to running the overall organization and include staff time spent in management, fund raising, bookkeeping, budget reporting, supervision, and other administrative tasks. It is easier to have a separate column for general operating costs and often enlightening to see how much it actually costs to keep the program running. However, it is difficult to raise funds separately for administration, and for proposal purposes you may wish to allocate administrative costs to each of the program areas for which you raise funds.

The third budget format is used for organizations that operate principally through a number of *branch offices*. Operating expenses are disbursed mainly according to office units, including the "home office." If there are some central expenses that apply to each of the units (such as administrative expenses), these should be distributed among the units according to appropriate proportions. Each office is accountable for meeting its budget.

Regardless of which format you use, as the year progresses, you and your board should review actual income and expenditures to date against some budget benchmark.

Cash Flow: Where Is Your Money When You Need It?

The budget tells you how much you expect to achieve in revenue and how much you will spend during a one-year period. However, there is another crucial piece of information you need: Will the money be available when you need to spend it? It is one thing to be able to say that you will raise $45,000 in a year to cover anticipated expenses of $45,000; it is another to have the cash in the bank when you have to pay your bills. In order to avoid a money crunch, you should develop a cash-flow chart that outlines anticipated expenses and income on a monthly basis.

Although most monthly expenses will be fairly steady month to month, some can fluctuate due to several factors: seasonal expenses, raises in salaries or rent, more or fewer staff members during a particular time of the year, one-time expenses (furniture, telephone installation, printing brochures), and so on. Thus, you need to anticipate how your expenses will be distributed monthly during the fiscal year. Also estimate when you will receive anticipated income from each of your identified sources: fees, grants, contracts, and so on.

Remember that fund raising takes time and that it will be months between an initial contact date and the actual receipt of money.

Outline anticipated income and expenses at least on a quarterly basis, preferably per month. If there appears to be a period when you will not have enough money to meet expenses, determine (1) whether it is realistic to anticipate that funds to cover these expenses will be available during a later period in the year, and (2) if so, whether you should cover these expenses with a loan to be repaid when the cash is available (remember the interest rates) or whether you can delay some of the expenses (furniture purchases can be delayed, salaries cannot); if not, you must determine how to cut back on your expenses.

The cash-flow schedule should also be used to compare estimated monthly expenses and income with the actual figures as the year progresses. If you have consistently overestimated your expected income or underestimated your expenses, you should determine why and take this into account when you prepare the next year's budget and cash-flow schedule.

When Should the Budget Be Revised?

Budget planning, especially for new organizations, is a difficult task, and some variances from the plan are likely. The monthly financial statements should include a comparison of budgeted revenue and expenses, by category or function, versus the actual results. The reasons for significant variances should be determined and reported to the board.

Generally, a budget should be revised *when it's clear that the variances will produce a result for the year that requires some action now for the good of the organization.* The staff relies on the budget to guide spending decisions. If an expense category must be reduced because of a shortfall in revenue, staff members need to be working with the revised numbers. However, because the board will want to know how well management planned for revenues and expenses, financial reports to the board should show both the original budget and any revised projections and reduced spending targets.

Sample Budget Format

Income Budget for Fiscal Year 199X

Earned Income

Fees from clients . . . . $

County contract . . . . $_____

    Total Earned Income . . . . $

Contributed Revenue

Anticipated cash grants . . . . $

Contributed equipment . . . . $

Fund raising benefits, net . . . . $_____

    Total Contributed Revenue . . . . $

    Total Income . . . . $

Expense Budget for Fiscal Year 199X

Human Resources

Salaries . . . . $

Temporary workers . . . . $

FICA, unemployment, benefits . . . . $

Staff development . . . . $

Physical Facility

Rent . . . . $

Utilities . . . . $

Janitorial services . . . . $

Equipment and maintenance . . . . $

Other Expenses

Insurance . . . . $

Loan repayments . . . . $

Supplies . . . . $

Postage . . . . $

Books/subscriptions . . . . $

Services purchased . . . . $

Printing . . . . $

Conferences and travel . . . . $

Miscellaneous and contingency . . . . $_____

    Total Expenses . . . . $

Budget Worksheet

This worksheet can be a useful tool. It will not only display total funds needed for each expense item, but also provide (1) detail of how you arrived at those costs and (2) a basis for developing a monthly cash-flow exhibit.

Expense Item	Calculation	Monthly	Annual
Compensation			
1. Executive director	Pay per period × number of periods monthly		
2.	As above		
3.	As above		
4.	As above		
Total Regular Wages		$	$
1. Temporary employees	$ per hour wage (or hourly rate of temporary agency) × average hours per month		
Total Temporaries		$	$
FICA, Unemployment, Benefits			
1. FICA/Medicare	% tax on salaries (to maximum per employee) × monthly salaries × number of employees		
2. Workers' comp	Insurance company quote		
3. State unemployment	% of salaries or other formula used in your state		
4. Health insurance	Average monthly premium per employee × number of employees		
5. Life insurance	Annual premium per employee × number of covered employees		
6. Retirement	Professional advice required		
7. Other benefits			
Total Benefits		$	$

Budget Worksheet *(continued)*

Expense Item	Calculation	Monthly	Annual
Staff Development	Could set an allowance per eligible employee or special identified needs; check local fees	$	$
Rent	Rate per month plus anticipated increase	$	$
Utilities (those not included in rent)			
1. Electricity	Ask utility to estimate monthly average or use "budget plan"		
2. Heat	As above		
3. Water	As above		
4. Telephone, local	Number of phones × monthly rate plus equipment costs		
5. Long-distance calls	Rate per minute for areas called often × minutes average call × estimated number of monthly calls		
Total Utilities		$	$
Janitorial services	Monthly charge	$	$
Equipment			
1. Purchased equipment	Estimate costs based on prices of several vendors		
2. Depreciation (reserve for eventual replacement)	Cost divided by estimated years of useful life		
3. Leased equipment	Contract price		
4. Maintenance	Monthly cost of maintenance contracts or ask repair firms to estimate maintenance costs		
Total Equipment		$	$

Budget Worksheet *(continued)*

Expense Item	Calculation	Monthly	Annual
Insurance	Secure quote for annual premiums	$	$
Loan Repayments	As stated in loan agreement	$	$
Supplies	Estimate supplies needed priced at office supply store	$	$
Postage	Estimate of weekly correspondence plus mass mailings plus annual bulk mail permit	$	$
Books and Subscriptions	Estimate of books and magazines needed	$	$
Services Purchased	As stated in service agreements	$	$
Printing	Monthly average per price list of commercial shop	$	$
Conferences	What's needed limited by what is affordable	$	$
Travel	Estimate number of miles staff usage of cars for job-related trips × mileage rate plus estimated parking fees plus air travel plus other local expenses	$	$
Advertising	Secure rate for likely size of ads from publications	$	$
Fees	Annual membership fees and licenses plus bank service fees	$	$
Total Expenses		$	$

Budget Worksheet *(continued)*

Income Item	Component	Monthly	Annual
Fees from Clients	Fee schedule × expected number of clients per month adjusted for seasonal variation	$	$
Government Contracts (list each contract)	Based on actual contract provisions	$	$
Contributed Revenue			
1. Cash grants	Best estimate based on fund raising research		
2. Contributed equipment	As above		
3. Event benefits	As above		
4. Individual contributions	As above		
5. Other	As above		
Total Contributed Income		$	$
Total Income		$	$

Accounting: Keeping Track of the $$$$

All organizations need workable systems for recording what they do with their money—keeping track of where it comes from and where it goes. On the other hand, young nonprofit agencies often are staffed by people unfamiliar with basic accounting methods. The purposes of this chapter are to introduce you to the types of records your agency will need, familiarize you with the elementary components of a bookkeeping system, define common accounting terms, explain that there are some differences in financial statements for nonprofits versus other kinds of organizations, and suggest how to obtain more comprehensive guidance on accounting and bookkeeping.

Setting Up an Accounting System

First of all—and this is probably the most important point of this chapter—do everything possible to commandeer the services of a willing and able accountant who will help you set up your bookkeeping system, teach you how to use it, and advise you about the most appropriate type of financial reporting for your organization. Board members, professional accounting associations, and business schools may be able to help you find a volunteer accountant or an affordable accounting service that specializes in serving nonprofits. (The search may not be easy, but it will be worth it, because it certainly helps a great deal to have some professional hand holding at this stage of the accounting game.)

After you have the books set up, you will need a bookkeeper. Very small or all-volunteer organizations may depend on the treasurer, who usually is a member of the board of directors, to fulfill this role on an unpaid basis. Medium-sized staffed organizations often rely on paid, specially trained secretaries to do the bookkeeping. Larger agencies sometimes hire part-time or full-time bookkeepers.

A good bookkeeping system provides the means for documenting, recording, summarizing, and reporting the financial transactions of your organization. A written record of your financial history is another benefit. Ultimately, you and your board should be able to use accounting information to make sound financial decisions and as an aid in future planning for your organization. The specific information that you get from a good bookkeeping system will do the following:

1. Tell you where your revenues came from and where they have been spent
2. Assist in budgeting and calculating fund raising needs
3. Assist in preventing the misuse of funds
4. Save money by identifying wasteful or inefficient spending
5. Provide the basis for determining the cost-effectiveness of each of your programs
6. Provide the information needed to construct required financial statements

Demands are placed upon an organization's administrators to provide detailed, accurate cost information about the services they provide. Funders, government bodies, clients, and consumer groups will ask for this information, and you must have the means of providing it. The future of your programs may depend on the quality of the financial information you can provide. The board of directors is responsible for ensuring that such information is available.

It is highly desirable to use an outside auditor — a CPA firm — to validate the financial information that is presented to your external publics, and some funders may require audited financial statements.

Many of the basic bookkeeping procedures commonly used by nonprofit organizations are similar to those used by commercial enterprises. However, nonprofit organizations are also required to follow some procedures that are unique to their type of operation and sources of revenue.

Accrual Accounting

One decision to be made is whether to use an "accrual" or a "cash" basis bookkeeping system. In a cash-base system, revenue is recorded when received (receipts) and expenses are recorded when paid (expenditures). In an accrual system, revenue is recorded *when it is earned*, which may be several months before or after it is actually received (that's when you wind up with "accounts receivable" for payments to come) and expenses are recorded *when they are incurred*, which may be before or after they are actually paid ("accounts payable" for payments still to be made and "prepaid expenses" for payments made before all of a given service has been provided to you).

In general, the information provided by an accrual bookkeeping system is more useful to an organization and anyone else with an interest in its financial condition than a cash system would be; accrual accounting provides a more accurate, total financial picture for a given period. Among other entries or adjustments, knowing both the amounts due to the organization and the amounts it owes to others means having more adequate information on which to base a financial assessment and to use in making financial projections. However, accrual systems are more complicated and time-consuming, which is disadvantageous to small nonprofits. An alternative is to keep the books on a cash basis, with an outside accountant helping you make accrual adjustments for year-end financial reports.

The Bookkeeping System

As stated earlier, bookkeeping procedures provide a means of documenting, recording, summarizing, and reporting your financial transactions. This section will address, very briefly, the basic components of a simple bookkeeping system.

Financial transactions, including cash receipts and cash disbursements, are recorded in chronological order in books called journals. Several types of journals may be kept by an organization, depending on the type of information that is to be recorded. All cash and checks received are entered in the *cash receipts journal* in columns with various headings under which you can record each item according to which type of income it is. All checks that you write from your operating account are entered in the *cash disbursements journal* under appropriate expense categories.

Your cash receipts journal should be used to back up the information that appears on your regular bank deposit statements. A receipt should be issued for each transaction. Bank deposits should be made regularly and frequently. Deposit slips should be made in duplicate, with a copy kept to assist in reconciling the bank account at the end of each month and for verification against the cash receipts journal.

It is important that all cash receipts be documented. (Not doing this is a common failing in record keeping among nonprofits.) Numbered receipts should be issued for all cash received; thank-you letters should be sent for all donations, and copies of them filed; and the vouchers or stubs of all checks received should be kept to document your deposits.

Also, your agency should get an endorsement stamp from the bank so that you can immediately endorse all checks when they are received in the mail. The endorsement stamp should read "For Deposit Only to the Account of [your organization's name]" and should include the bank account number and the name of the bank. Alternatively, and especially if you receive a large number of checks as the result of fund raising campaigns, you can have the checks sent directly to the bank by the use of a lock box. This provides stronger protection against theft or misuse of funds. Even in the smallest organizations, it is recommended that cash and checks be received and the mail opened by someone other than the person who makes the deposits. A separate list of all the checks and cash received should be kept by this person on a daily basis, and a copy of the list should be passed on to the bookkeeper. This control mechanism is very important, but it is all too often overlooked in agencies that feel they do not have sufficient staff. In addition, if possible, the person who touches the cash should not also touch the books.

Your cash disbursements journal is used to record all of the checks that you write. You must document why each check was written. When it is appropriate, documentation should include a copy of the bill covered by the check. The bill should be marked with the date, check number, and amount paid. If there is no bill, there should be a simple request form that agency staff members can use to request checks for items such as postage, conference preregistration, and mileage reimbursement. This form should include date, amount, payee, reason for payment, the name of the person requesting the check, and the signature of someone authorized to approve the expenditure. Your organization should have a procedure whereby all purchases are authorized for payment before checks are written. If this is not possible, the executive director should personally initial all bills before signing the checks for payment.

For control reasons, it is best that all operating checking accounts require two signatures for checks, but at least two signatures should always be required for large amounts ("large" for a very small nonprofit might be $50 or more; for a larger nonprofit, $1,000 or $2,000 or more). The usual method is to require that both the executive director and one of the corporate officers of the board of directors sign checks. In the absence of the executive director, two of the other designated officers sign. Relevant documents, such as the original bills or request forms, should be presented with the checks for signature.

The cash receipts journal and the cash disbursements journal are used to record money received and money spent, but if there is a paid staff, a separate payroll journal should be kept that records the amount earned by each employee, the amount withheld for taxes, the amount paid for benefits, and the amount paid to the employee. Sales or fees-earned journals should also be kept when this type of income is received regularly by your agency. An accrual-basis accounting system also requires an *accounts receivable journal* and an *accounts payable journal.*

The procedures outlined above concern the documenting and recording functions of the bookkeeping system. The summarizing function is performed by the *general ledger.* This is a book with a separate sheet for each category of assets (bank accounts, petty cash, accounts receivable, furniture and equipment), liabilities (accounts payable, loans), income (grants, contracts, fees), and expenses (rent, salaries, supplies, and so on). At the end of each month, all of the entries in your journals are totaled and the total for each category of expenses and income is entered onto the appropriate page of the general ledger. Each of these categories is called an *account*. In order to save time and make record keeping easier, each account is usually assigned a number. The list of these numbered accounts is referred to as the *chart of accounts*.

Accounting software is available for various types of personal computers, and there are several programs that are relatively easy to use (well, at least you don't have to be an accounting professional to use them).

Financial Accounting Standards

The Financial Accounting Standards Board sets the accounting standards for various types of organizations, including nonprofits. Its standards are labeled by FASB number, for example, FASB 117 (FASB is pronounced FAZbee). You can put together financial reports in various ways to satisfy internal requirements, but three particular annual financial statement approaches are required by FASB to focus attention on the organization as a whole: the statement of financial position, the statement of activities (your annual operating statement), and the statement of cash flows.

Statement of Financial Position

If you ever learned the most basic accounting concepts, you probably knew the statement of financial position as a "balance sheet." It shows "assets" (what you own, such as cash, investments, facilities and equipment), "liabilities" (what you owe or other financial obligations, such as loans you've taken out and accounts payable), and "net assets" (what's left after you subtract liabilities from assets).

The minimum information that should be displayed in this statement is the total net assets broken down into unrestricted, temporarily restricted, and permanently restricted. As the name implies, an unrestricted net asset can be spent as you (or your board) decides. A temporarily restricted net asset is one that can be used only for a certain purpose for a certain period of time—for example, earnings from an endowment that can be used only for a designated purpose for a certain number of years. A permanently restricted net asset is one that can never be used for anything but a designated purpose.

Statement of Activities

At a minimum, your statement of activities (your annual operating statement) should show the change in net assets during the past year for the organization as a whole, the change in each of the three classes of net assets mentioned above, and whether any items were moved from one net asset class to another.

Statement of Cash Flows

The statement of cash flows provides information about the cash receipts and cash disbursements of the organization. In addition, donors' pledges (unconditional promises to contribute) must be included in the financial statements in the years the pledges were made. Thus, if your nonprofit receives a three-year grant commitment from a foundation, the entire three-year sum must be recognized as revenue on your financial statements in the year of the promise. If, however, the foundation indicates only an intention to give, with no actual pledge, this does not constitute a promise.

An example would be a promise to match other grants you are able to secure. In addition, pledges will need to be adjusted for the time value of money and the likelihood of collectibility. (*Time value*, also called *present value*, means that a dollar in hand today is worth more than a dollar you get a year from now. You can invest the dollar if you have it today and earn interest on it. Adjusting the value of pledges for their time value and collectibility is something to discuss with that accounting expert you're going to try to commandeer as a volunteer!)

Copies of FASB standards may be secured from FASB's Order Department, 401 Meritt 7, P.O. Box 5116, Norwalk, CT 16856, or from an accounting firm, which can also provide you with sample exhibits *currently being used by nonprofit organizations* (see also the bibliography).

Accounting for Donated Services and Materials

Nonprofit agencies depend heavily on time donated by volunteers and contributed supplies and equipment. In many instances, an organization could not carry out its operations without these "in-kind" contributions. It is important, therefore, that your agency account for such contributions in order to provide a total picture of the costs of your services.

As a rule of thumb, you should include in your financial records and reports those contributed items or services for which you otherwise would have had to pay and without which you would be unable to function. Common examples are donated office space and equipment and use of another organization's printing and copying machines.

In order to count these materials and services as contributions and then as expenses in your program, you must do three things: (1) be able to document that you did receive them, (2) assign realistic values to them, and (3) have total control over them once they are donated to you. Accounts of donated material and services not only show the total costs of your program, they also provide excellent public relations tools. Such figures show funders the interest in your organization that others have expressed through donation of time and materials.

Incidentally, volunteer *fund raising* efforts usually are not recorded, because they do not directly fulfill the organization's objectives or provide services to clients.

Functional Program Accounting

Functional program accounting is a bookkeeping/accounting method, also known as *cost accounting*, in which costs are assigned to each of the programs an agency may run and to its management and fund raising functions. Program accounting is designed to answer the question: How much does it cost to operate program A and program B? How much is spent on fund raising? On agency administration? Accounting for each program's costs separately helps you to have a complete financial picture of your organization and to determine the "unit cost" of each program, such as the cost of serving each client or the cost of one hour's service. Such information allows you (and funders) to compare the cost of your program to similar ones in the community, and it allows you to see the results of your fund raising efforts in relationship to their costs. It also allows for better budgeting for future needs.

Increasingly, funders, government bodies, and various auditing agents are requiring that the organizations they audit follow program accounting methods. (If your organization expects to secure more than $100,000 per year in federal funds, in which case certain prescribed federal audits are required, the federal rules are very specific about allowable methods of cost allocation. Failing to do so can cost you big bucks!)

Assigning costs requires carefully followed procedures and detailed record keeping: maintaining detailed time records for employees, having purchases authorized by program supervisors so that the bookkeepers know how to charge the costs when checks are written, and determining how office space is actually used by your program. Many costs are then allocated on the basis of percentage of time spent or space used in a given function.

Detailed, consistent record keeping by all employees is essential if you are to account for the costs of each of your programs. It's not uncommon for staff people to resist preparing the detailed paperwork that such a system demands; the agency administrator should explain the importance of such cost analysis as an aid to providing better and more effective services to the agency's constituency. If staff members are involved in program planning and budgeting, they are likely to be more willing and able to document income and spending appropriately.

Financial Reports: Telling It Like It Is

It is from the summary of your financial transactions in the general ledger that you prepare financial reports. In addition to the financial statements established by FASB, as outlined earlier in this chapter, your reports may take many forms, depending on the organization and its internal needs and the needs of interested persons and organizations outside the agency. No matter how many or how few, how simple or how complex your financial reports are, there are some general criteria to follow.

Financial Reports Should Be Clear

Any person taking the time to read one of your financial reports should be able to understand it. Understandable titles, clear descriptions, and simple format are essential. In-house jargon or codes that would not be understood by someone outside the organization should not be used.

Financial Reports Should Be Consistent

The same methods and the same way of presenting information should be used every time a particular report is produced.

Financial Reports Should Be Concise

Reports should be kept as short as possible, so that no one will get lost in detail. There is nothing wrong with presenting two or three short reports rather than one long, detailed one. In some cases, you may wish to distribute one report or set of reports to the public and reserve a more detailed set for your board of directors.

Financial Reports Should Be All-Inclusive

Your financial reports should provide a total picture of all the activities of your organization. Reporting on separate programs and funds is important. Even when you keep your books on a cash basis, every effort should be made to include accrued income and expenses in these reports to give a full picture of your financial position. In other words, periodic financial reports should report income earned or pledged but not yet received and debts owed but not yet paid.

Financial Reports Should Be Comparable

Your reports should have some point for comparison so that the reader will have a basis for arriving at some conclusion about your financial activity over a period of time.

This can be in comparison to planned budget figures or to amounts from a corresponding period of time in the previous year.

Financial Reports Should Be Timely

Reports should be issued on a regular (monthly or quarterly) basis, and they should be prepared as soon after the end of the period as possible. Otherwise, they lose their significance and usefulness.

You Must Know What Financial Reports Are Required

Nonprofit organizations may be required by state law to submit annual financial reports. This requirement may depend on the amount received in annual contributions and other revenue. Your state may or may not require that any annual financial report be prepared by a certified public accountant. The state department of commerce can tell you whether or not you are required to submit an annual financial report. An annual audit by a CPA is also required by some funders, and this can be a helpful financial review for an organization itself. Your board members or an accounting aid association, if there is one in your city, may be able to help you understand how to prepare for an audit and how to select a firm to do it. You may even get help in locating volunteer or low-cost accounting services.

You, Your Board, and Your Money

Proper use of your money is safeguarded by a number of financial control practices within your organization. The usual term used to refer to these is *internal control*. As you have seen, internal control takes many forms, such as dual-signature checks, approval of expenditures, and controlled handling of cash. In addition, governance (your board of directors) plays a very important role in financial control. Final legal responsibility for your organization rests in this body. Too often, simple steps for guaranteeing the board's input and the ultimate responsibility of the board are forgotten.

The fiduciary responsibility of the board of directors includes the review and approval of written financial management guidelines and policies (such as requiring an annual balanced budget and a certain cash reserve) and guidelines for entering into contracts and leases. The board should discuss and approve your agency's budget (this could also include the participation of a board committee in the preparation of the budget). The board also should discuss and approve your agency's periodic financial reports. All contracts should be approved by the board, and they should be signed by a board officer and the executive director. A written limit should be placed on the dollar amount and types of expenditures that can be authorized by your executive director without board approval, and all other expenses should be approved by the board, with documentation in the minutes of the board's meeting. A board member should approve all payments for personal expenses incurred by the executive director.

An audit of your books should be conducted annually, and the auditor should, independent of the staff, report the results of the audit to the board of directors.

Don't minimize the board's financial involvement and responsibility by bypassing the procedures outlined above. Requiring the board's knowledge of financial operations and involvement in financial decision making can ensure effective control of your organization's money.

Fund Raising: Finding the $$$$

What kind of funding strategy will keep your organization operating effectively? Who will fund your activities? How do you successfully approach potential funders—foundations, corporations, other businesses, government, and individuals? Will you focus on annual giving by foundations, corporations, and individuals, or will you also use special events, try to create an endowment, or establish a "planned giving" program?

This chapter is an introduction to fund raising strategy, developing funding sources, and soliciting contributions. The information included in this chapter does not reflect everything that could be said about philanthropy and how to raise funds, but this book's bibliography lists some valuable books and other materials that will help you. Most of the reference books listed are available in the Foundation Center collections located in more than eighty libraries throughout the United States—useful starting points for research on fund raising. For more information on the Foundation Center, see "Sources of Assistance" in the back of this book. You should also call other nonprofit organizations to find out if useful seminars on fund raising are available in your area.

Writing grant proposals, soliciting contributions from individuals, and other fund raising techniques are crucial skills that most new nonprofit organizations must acquire early in their development. Both the board of directors and the executive director of the organization should be active in fund raising. Other volunteers can be trained to help as well, especially in soliciting donations from individuals. A sound strategy, research to identify realistic prospects, and an investment of time and energy to learn the basics of fund raising will be critical to your success.

Funding Strategies

You need dollars for general operating expenses—rent, utilities, administration, and so on. You require money to run your specific programs—art shows, social services, educational courses, whatever. You may need financial help dedicated to short-term projects—strategic planning, setting up a computer system, surveys. And someday you may undertake a capital campaign—raising money for your own building or an endowment fund—and you may establish a planned giving program. (An *endowment fund* consist of assets contributed by one or more wealthy individuals and/or a number of foundations and corporations. The assets are invested to produce annual income available for general operating expense or designated uses. *Planned giving* involves a major gift that fits a particular donor's financial needs, e.g., a way to make a major contribution to a favorite charity through a will, living trust, life insurance, annuity, or other means.)

To raise money, you must identify the best sources for each type of financial need. You've probably been on the receiving end of standard, mass-mailed letters asking for your personal donation. That kind of approach will not work with foundations, corporations, government, and other institutional funders. And even mass mailings to individuals generally target people who have been identified as having potential interest in the appeal.

Some institutional funders (foundations, businesses, associations, and government) will provide ongoing general operating support; some want to provide grants only for programs; some will never make capital grants; and some will consider all of the above. Some funders focus on a few charitable areas, such as the arts, neighborhood development, youth services, education, protecting the environment, or human rights advocacy.

Most funders have written guidelines as to what they will fund and how you can apply for grants. Many foundations and corporations with major charitable giving programs issue annual reports, which generally list actual grants. Do your homework, so that your time and resources are focused on funders most likely to be interested in your programs.

Individual donors who respond favorably to what you're doing and who you serve are usually a good source of funds for general operating support.

Both as you first devise your strategy and periodically thereafter, try to see yourself as funders may. Place yourself in the position of those with the money to give and review what you are telling potential funders about your organization and its programs. Would you be impressed? Honestly, now—impressed enough to give some dollars?

Listed below are the critical questions you will need to ask yourself as you devise your fund raising strategies (much of this should already be included in your organization's strategic plan).

Has Your Program Been Clearly Defined and the Community Need Documented?

Have you clearly described the mission of your organization (in other words, the reason it exists) as well as its vision (what it intends to be), the purpose and goals of its programs, and how you pursue those goals? Does the program for which you are soliciting funding really fulfill a significant need in the community?

Does Your Program Duplicate Services Offered Elsewhere?

Show that you are aware of any other organizations that are working in your problem area and explain why your program offers something of value not otherwise available or show that the need is great enough to warrant an additional nonprofit to serve that need.

If you have coordinated your program with other agencies, be sure to say that. Your referral and resource network should be outlined. If you are duplicating services provided by others in order to demonstrate alternative methods or strategies, explain the differences in your approach to the problem and why those differences are worth funding.

Has the Credibility of Your Agency Been Established?

This is a highly subjective judgment on the part of the funder. One measurement of reliability is your track record, if you have one; that is, how has your program performed in the past? If, as is likely given that you're reading this book, your organization is new, what other efforts have you (the staff, volunteers, and board members) been involved with that relate to the mission of your organization and the services you provide? Who in the community supports your project? Have you involved the potential users of your programs in designing those programs?

Who Is Involved?

This is closely related to your credibility. Who are your staff members (paid or volunteer)? The ability of the staff to carry out the program and of the board to direct the organization responsibly and raise funds necessary for ongoing support should be explained. Who is serving on your board of directors? Information about board members' corporate or other affiliations will be of interest to many potential funders.

Exactly what the board's role in fund raising will be needs to be resolved. Board members may be most effective in helping to raise money from individuals and in helping you make contacts with institutional funders.

Is the Proposed Budget Realistic?

Does your budget provide funds sufficient to accomplish your program's objectives and yet reflect your cost consciousness?

Where Else Are You Seeking Funds?

Most funders are reluctant to be the sole source of support for a nonprofit. Your proposal should indicate who else you are approaching, demonstrating your attempt to involve a range of funding sources. Will the contribution of this funder stimulate giving by others? (Often, one or two funders in a community are viewed as leaders in philanthropy by other funders; securing a grant from such a funder can open doors to others.)

What Are Your Future Funding Plans?

If your project is to be ongoing, how will the program be maintained when currently requested funds run out? Many funders (especially foundations) don't want you leaning on their shoulders too long. If you don't have confirmed plans, you should at least indicate that you have been contacting possible sources for future funding. Discuss whether you charge fees for your services, including who pays the fees, how much the fees are, and whether or not you use a sliding scale based on clients' financial resources or other factors.

What Changes Will Your Program Make in Your Clients? In Your Community?

Have you developed specific, measurable objectives? Clearly describe, in quantitative terms, the changes you want to facilitate in your clients and in the community. Make sure that these projected outcomes are realistic. You must have measurable objectives in order to evaluate the effectiveness of your program.

How Will You Know Whether You Have Accomplished Your Objectives?

The criteria you plan to use to monitor your progress should be described in your proposal. Develop an evaluation process. Will the evaluation be internal or involve outside consultants? What instruments and forms, if any, will you use? An evaluation plan will not only give your funders a means of judging your effectiveness, but more important, it will allow you to refine and improve your program as it develops.

The Case Statement

A case statement explains why your organization exists and why it should be funded. The answers to the above questions will help develop the statement, which should include the following:

- An overall, clear (but concise) description of the organization —
  when founded, why, mission, vision, and any unique characteristics. You should be able to take this right from your strategic
  plan.
- An outline of the population and geographic area served, the
  services or programs provided, how provided, growth, recent
  developments, and any evaluations of the impacts your services
  or programs are having. Document the needs of your target
  population for the services you will provide and the extent to
  which your program will respond to those needs. Indicate how
  you assessed these needs, such as through a survey, other research, interviews, or government data. Beware of jargon and
  be sure to define your terms.
- A list of the resources required to fund your organization and
  its programs. Include any actual or expected "earned income,"
  that is, money you earn from ticket sales, fees, merchandise,
  and the like. List existing funders.
- Information on the board of directors, other volunteerism,
  and any sponsorships, endorsements, or affiliations with other
  organizations.

The reader of the case statement should be able to understand exactly what your organization is all about, its importance to the community, how it operates, who it serves, and why the reader should care about enhancing your capacity to achieve your mission. It will be your principal source document for developing grant proposals, recruiting a board of directors and other volunteers, and communicating with the community.

Funding Sources

Foundations

There are more than twenty-seven thousand active U.S. foundations (which are also tax-exempt nonprofits). Some foundations are huge; some are small. Some focus on one or a few types of programs; some are willing to fund a broad range of nonprofit en-deavors. Foundations don't fund only big nonprofits. Increasingly, many are funding smaller projects serving low-income neighborhoods or other grassroots efforts. Regardless of size or program interest, foundations tend to fall into one of the following categories.

Independent Foundations: Most foundations fall into this category. Independent foundations may be local or national in scope, and their endowments may have come from an individual, family, or group of people. They may have a broad charter for grantsmaking, but many limit their giving to well-defined program areas. They may have large, full-time staffs and prestigious boards of directors drawn from the community, or the founding family may control governance and giving.

Within this broad category are such large, national, wide-reaching foundations as the Ford Foundation, the Rockefeller Foundation, and the Carnegie Foundation (despite the large scope of these foundations, they do not necessarily exclude small local organizations from consideration for grants); special purpose foundations, established usually through a will or a trust to give money to one specific cause — a scholarship fund or a specific college, for example; and so-called family foundations, established by wealthy individuals, including highly successful entrepreneurs, or families, which fund charitable programs according to the donors' wishes (local institutions and causes favored by the donors are the usual beneficiaries) and often governed by family members.

Community Foundations: These are professionally staffed foundations that receive money from many local sources (smaller family foundations, gifts, and estates) and distribute it to local causes. One staff, then, does the work for many funding sources and small foundations. Community foundations are usually governed by boards made up of prominent local citizens.

Although most of the funds handled by community foundations are designated for specific beneficiaries or service areas, often these foundations have some open-ended and unrestricted funds available for other causes. A wide variety of programs are supported by community foundations, due to the broad range of their donors' interests. The oldest community foundations in the United States are the Minneapolis Foundation and the Cleveland Foundation.

Corporate Foundations: Corporate foundations are separate legal organizations set up with their own assets by business corporations. Although legally independent of the sponsoring company, the corporate foundation is generally governed by trustees who are also company officers. A corporate foundation often focuses its contributions in communities where the corporation operates and in service areas of interest to the corporation or its employees.

Foundations of any kind almost always have printed guidelines available that cover what they fund, how to apply for grants, and so on.

Corporations and Other Businesses

Many corporations operate direct-giving programs, funded by annual pretax earnings, rather than make grants from corporate foundations (some do both). Often these grants are administered by professional staff who sometimes work in the corporation's "community relations," "public affairs," or "public relations" department. They may fund a broad range of charities where the company has branches; focus only or principally on the corporation's headquarters city; make grants without any geographic limitation; consider any kind of charity; focus on business-related interests; or make grants independent of the corporation's business interests but give preference to one type of giving, such as the arts, education, or a particular type of human service. As with foundations, corporations' giving functions generally have printed guidelines available that cover what they are willing to consider funding.

Other businesses—accounting and law firms, retailers, small and medium-sized manufacturers and service businesses—may also make charitable contributions, and some will offer pro bono services (professional services provided without charge), in-kind gifts (such as a computer manufacturer providing free or heavily discounted equipment), or other noncash contributions (e.g., used furniture or other equipment a company is replacing, printing services).

Membership Organizations

Membership organizations—such as service clubs (Kiwanis, Lions), fraternal organizations (Elk, Moose), civic/business associations (chambers of commerce), professional societies (bar associations), and women's organizations—also donate funds to projects of interest to them. The proposal process for seeking funding from such organizations usually is less formal and more personal than the process required by larger funders. Generally, such organizations give small amounts to local community and neighborhood projects. A good way to access these sources of funds is to offer to make presentations on the community needs your program serves at these groups' periodic membership meetings.

Religious Groups

Citywide and national units of churches, synagogues, and other religious groups can also be important sources of funding for some programs.

Federated Fund Drives

United Way and other combined appeals annually conduct a centralized fund raising campaign among individuals, businesses, and foundations and disburse these funds to affiliated agencies. Although usually affiliated with the national United Way, each community United Way organization functions autonomously. Larger United Way organizations have full-time, professional staffs and are governed by a board of directors composed of community members. In addition to fund raising, larger United Way units also provide planning and coordination for member agencies. In addition, some provide some management support and program evaluation services to member agencies.

Generally, the application process for becoming part of a United Way or other combined appeal must begin at least a year before the next funding period. Although new agencies may apply for membership in most of these federated fund drives, only a small amount of funding generally is given to agencies and programs in their early stages of development.

An agency that receives money from a federated fund drive may be required to participate in public presentations of the fund drive, have an agency representative serve on a committee, or provide other support.

Contributions by Individuals

Developing individual gifts can take a greater investment of time, and sometimes money, than securing grants from foundations, corporations, and other institutions, but such gifts are often more stable than grant funding over the long haul.

Public Funding Sources

On the other side of the coin is government funding. Many nonprofit agencies receive some, most, or all of their money from one or more government units. Government funding is available at several levels—federal, state, county, and city.

Public funding differs significantly from private funding in the proposal process, accountability requirements, and guideline compliance (e.g., in the area of hiring practices). Public funding takes one of several forms:

> *Grants:* funds awarded by a government unit to private institutions or state or local units of government for the support of programs originated and defined by the agencies themselves. Project grants provide funds for service delivery, research, training, technical assistance, facilities, and equipment.
>
> *Contracts:* funds awarded by a government unit to public or private agencies through contracts, which are legal agreements, to purchase assistance in carrying out its own program goals. Such assistance can include surveys and studies, evaluation services, human resource services, consulting, training, conferences, and production of publications and other materials.
>
> *Request for Proposal (RFP):* solicitation of proposals for a grant or a contract for a specific service or activity outlined by the RFP.

Purchase of Service: a means by which a government agency, rather than delivering services directly with its own employees, can provide for delivery by contracting with private agencies to provide the services. The government unit, in effect, buys services for its clients from private agencies through purchase of service agreements.

It may be harder to figure out the most appropriate public funding source from which to seek support than it is to choose which private resources to approach. Maintaining informal contacts and keeping up-to-date on funding activities related to your field are especially important. In addition, you should do the following:

- Find out which local and state government units relate to your service area. If they issue newsletters, get on the mailing list.
- Know and contact legislators (both state and federal) on key related committees.
- Identify and attend conferences in your field (local, regional, and, if possible, national). The contacts you make there can be invaluable.
- Talk to others from similar programs who have recently received public funding.

Fees for Service

This type of funding is more appropriate for some types of programs than for others, depending on the clients involved and the services offered. In some cases, third-party fee payment is possible. For instance, payment for chemical dependency treatment may be covered by the medical insurance of the client. Other programs charge fees according to a sliding fee scale based on the client's income and ability to pay. Sales of publications produced by an organization are also considered fees for service, as an organization's membership fees may be.

Fees for service usually constitute only a small portion of a nonprofit organization's projected income because of the objective of providing services to those who need them, regardless of their ability to pay. Nevertheless, private and public funding sources often want the programs they support to charge fees, however small, to those clients who can afford them.

Developing Grant Proposals

Planning

The first step in looking for funding is to ask yourself the simple question stated earlier, which you must keep constantly in mind: Is the program you are proposing truly worth funding? You must have not just a worthwhile idea, but a well-planned and carefully defined program that will appeal to others. Potential funders must be able to get a clear understanding of what it is you are asking them to support.

The case statement, outlined earlier, is your starting point for developing the grant proposal along the lines of what each potential funder has established as what it wants included in applications for grants. Throughout the early planning stage, write down key points and ideas that may be useful during proposal writing. Proposals should be written only after the purpose and scope of the program have been carefully delineated, its relationship to existing community resources outlined, and methods and target population defined.

During the planning stage, you also should gather documentation of the needs that your program proposes to meet. Such documentation should include demographic and census data related to your service area that give basic information about your target population (age, education, income, and so on) and the extent of the problems you are addressing (rates of drug abuse, unemployment and crime, extent of deteriorated housing, degree of environmental damage, or whatever). Such data are available from state, county, and city departments in the areas of health, welfare, crime and delinquency, planning, recreation, and law enforcement. Private agencies that serve the same target population you will also should be able to give you information in these areas. Any studies and reports, especially local ones, that are related to your program area may also provide documentation.

In addition, outline the services currently available to your potential constituency. What services will you provide that differ from those already available? How will your program interact with these? Your program will not be viewed in isolation; it will be considered as part of a network of services and programs. You must be able to explain where your organization will fit into that network.

Contact other persons involved in your field, especially those whose agencies your program will be working with, receiving referrals from, and making referrals to. Other support and input should be solicited from related bodies or from legislators. Get this input early in the planning process and identify those people who support your proposed program and are willing to serve as references for potential funders. Solicit letters of support from such contacts.

You need to follow these steps if you are going to persuade funders that your proposal is necessary and worthwhile and ensure that you develop a program that will be effective and responsive to the needs of those you serve. If you cannot persuade any funders that your program is worthwhile, it may not be!

Identifying Potential Funding Sources

Identify the funders that seem the most likely possibilities. You can use the directories and other resources described in the bibliography to develop a list of possible funders for your program. Once you have your list, telephone or write for copies of the funders' guidelines for grantsmaking and annual reports of their giving (not all funders produce annual reports, but those that do usually list the organizations to whom they have made grants).

Does your program fall within their interest areas? Have they funded similar programs? Do your funding needs fit within the range of their average grant size? Is the timing of their grantsmaking process favorable (or will you just miss a once-a-year deadline)?

Next, narrow your list to several likely possibilities. For each of these sources, study (1) the application procedures and deadlines if any (it is important to follow the guidelines exactly in preparing your proposal); (2) the reporting requirements, if funded; (3) how granting decisions are made and by whom; and (4) the likelihood that you could develop a good working relationship with this funding source.

It is important to consider the side effects that can come with funding from some sources. Occasionally, funders try to exert control over the programs they fund and require changes. Some (government funding units, in particular) require extensive reporting and conformity to specific guidelines. Such side effects can require much time and some compromise on your part. Your group must decide whether the requirements of a particular funding source are acceptable.

Write each source a letter outlining your program (form letters should never be used), explaining who you are, what you plan to do, how you will do it, and how much it will cost, and asking for the opportunity to present a complete proposal for your program. If you can arrange it, a personal meeting with the funding source could take the place of this initial letter. If not, follow up your letter with a telephone call to request a face-to-face meeting. This initial contact is important. You can save time and money if you can avoid sending proposals to funding sources that are not interested or for which you do not qualify.

If the funding source is interested, elicit advice about your proposal's content, format, and length and any other suggestions that may improve your chances of obtaining funding.

Finalizing and Submitting Proposals

The length of a proposal should generally be related to the amount of money requested. For instance, don't submit a twenty-five-page proposal for a $3,000 budget. Small grant requests need only short proposals, although most of the areas outlined should be briefly addressed.

Most of the information to be included in your proposal should have been gathered during your early planning stages. After the proposal has been written, test it out on someone else—a few concerned (and frank) critics who will read the proposal and offer suggestions. (The chapters in this volume on planning and budgeting will also be helpful for proposal planning.)

As noted earlier, many of the places to which you will send proposals (foundations, corporations, and government agencies, in particular) will have application forms that must be completed. Some may merely outline broadly what the proposal should include. Be sure you have the most recent proposal guidelines and application forms. Usually, the guidelines will ask you to include the following sections.

Overview: Briefly summarize your program, who you are, what you propose to do, and how much money you need. This could be in the form of a cover letter. The summary is important because it is the first thing the funding source will read and it may be used for an initial screening process. This is where you first "sell" your program to your potential funding source.

Organization's Qualifications: In the body of the proposal, describe the background and history of your organization, your community support, and the past accomplishments of your organization or of your staff and board members. The proposal should explain how the organization got started and why. Letters of support from key community members and representatives of other agencies can be included in an appendix. Copies of any newspaper articles about your program or those involved in it can also be included.

Problem or Need: Document the problem: the existing conditions, their scope, and their impact on the community. You should refer to important statistics, related reports, surveys, and assessments of the problem by community representatives and professionals in the field. The problem should be defined in terms of what your program can realistically address. If the problem appears too overwhelming to funders, they will feel that your program and the money they put into it will never be able to have an impact on the problem. You should be specific as to what you think your impact on the problem will be.

Goals and Objectives: Your proposal should describe the intended outcomes of your program and its effect on the problem you have described. Again, you must be realistic. Your objectives should be achievable. They should also be measurable, and they should refer to the changes that will be brought about through your program. The goals and objectives should follow directly from your definition of the problem. You must not confuse methods with objectives. (You should be able to extract the goals and objectives from your strategic plan.)

Methods or Strategies: Statements of objectives speak about outcomes; statements of methods or strategies describe the processes or means used to reach objectives. Outline the activities you will conduct to accomplish your objectives, including a timetable, if possible. You should include your rationale for using particular methods instead of others. (Again, these strategies should already be in your strategic plan.)

Staff: Your proposal should include a description of the responsibilities and qualifications of the program's staff and may outline the structure of the organization (include an organizational chart of decision-making processes).

Evaluation: Describe how you will measure your program's effectiveness and whether or not you have achieved your goals and objectives. Indicate whether the evaluation will be conducted in-house or whether you will use an outside consultant.

Future Funding: If the funding source is not being asked to fund the entire program, where will the rest of the funding come from? Outline your present and future plans for funding. Funders look for a well-planned funding strategy that indicates you are not permanently or totally dependent upon them and that you have thought out your funding future realistically.

Budget: The proposal should list your anticipated expenditures, including salaries and benefits, rent, utilities, equipment, supplies, and so on. It should also outline projected income. The budget should be realistic. Are you trying to run a $100,000 program on a $50,000 budget? Or are you asking for $100,000 for a program that could be conducted for $50,000? If your objectives and methods do not match the scope of your budget, your credibility could be damaged.

Appendix: Copies of your letters of support, staff résumés, list of board members, letter of tax exemption (a must), and any statistical charts and newspaper clippings about your organization should be attached to your proposal as an appendix.

Cover Letter: Proposals should be typed and accompanied by a personal cover letter addressed to the director of the funding source. It is acceptable to submit identical proposals to a number of funders at the same time. Each proposal, however, should ask for a specific amount of money. You should not ask each funder for the total amount needed. As noted above, most funders do not wish to be your sole source of support.

The cover letter should indicate any other sources from which you are seeking funds, any sources who have supported you in the past, and your long-range funding plans (many sources do not want to fund you forever). You may also suggest a meeting to discuss your request, but although personal contact is the best way to sell your program, don't be surprised if the funder's staff are unwilling to make a "site visit" (i.e., come out to your agency to see how your program operates) or to allow you to make a personal visit to their office. Many funders are short staffed, considering what is expected of them (just like nonprofits!) and, given the scads of applications sent to them, just don't have the time to meet with everyone seeking grants.

Follow-up

Many funders will acknowledge receipt of your proposal. If you hear nothing within a couple of weeks after you have submitted a proposal, you may call the funder to be sure it arrived. (However, the staff generally will not appreciate calls asking about the *status* of your request while it is under consideration.) The decision-making process may be a lengthy one from your point of view. The funder's guidelines probably will at least hint at the time-line, which may range from a few weeks to several months. If you don't hear of the funder's decision when expected, then follow up with a telephone call.

If funds are not granted, ask the funder to explain the reasons for the rejection and, if it is appropriate, ask whether you can resubmit your proposal at a different point in your organization's development.

If you receive a grant, be sure you understand the reporting procedures you are expected to follow. In some cases, periodic progress reports are required. Otherwise, reporting is usually left to your discretion. You should be prepared to give your funding sources information about program activities (especially any major changes in the program), expenditures, staff changes, and any other relevant data. Even if they do not specifically require it, send your program's annual reports to all your funding sources. It is important to develop good ongoing relationships with your funders. They can be an important source for ideas regarding program development, future funding, and community support. In addition, they can be used as references about your program when you approach other funding sources in the future.

Getting Donations from Individuals

Developing a base of annual individual contributors to your program requires a lot of work and the investment of some money, but if you have a program that appeals to the general public, or to individuals with a special interest that coincides with your mission, you can develop a dependable, steady source of money for general operating expenses.

Methods

There are a number of ways to secure contributions from individuals. Determining which ones will produce the best results for your organization and which you have the resources to support will involve a lot of thought by you and your board. You may want to set up a special committee to research, design, and oversee this effort.

Memberships: Many 501(c)(3) nonprofits have members. Some members may have voting rights, but more often the members are simply donors with no other role to play. Unless they receive something of value as part of their membership, their dues generally are tax deductible. (An "incidental" benefit, such as a token mug, key chain, or poster, does not necessarily reduce the deduction. Publications generally are considered by the IRS to have no measurable fair market value if their primary purpose is to inform members about organizational activities and if they're not available to nonmembers by paid subscription or newsstand sales. But if an organization's publication includes articles written for pay and accepts advertising, it could be treated as a "commercial quality" publication having a measurable market value. The IRS rules change from time to time, so secure the latest rules from the IRS.)

Annual Fund: This is usually an annual solicitation, but it may be conducted throughout the year. Some nonprofits use the annual fund drive not only to secure dollars but to recruit volunteers. High-income people who have special interest in your work can be sources of substantial annual gifts.

Planned Giving: Federal and state income tax laws can make bequests attractive ways for a person with investments and other assets to make sizable gifts to favored charities.

Special Events: Fund raising dinners, auctions, and festivals are among the numerous ways that many nonprofits have developed to encourage individuals to provide financial support. Special events can also help you build a mailing list of people interested in the mission of your organization that you can use for annual fund solicitations.

Develop a Step-by-Step Process

Raising money from individuals, like any other fund raising effort, involves a step-by-step process.

1. You still need to develop the case statement for your program—Why should a donor care enough to part with some dollars to support your cause?—but appeals to individuals require a more concise approach than do those to institutional

funders. Often, "anecdotal" material works well with individuals—telling the story of a typical user of your service.

2. What kinds of people will find your cause appealing? (First, of course, should be your board of directors and other volunteers already involved with your organization. They also may be able to suggest other people who may be willing to contribute.) Identify the "audience" with the greatest potential ties to your program and that would seem to have the greatest potential to give. Then identify others with some connection to your cause and who might have some interest and ability to give. Continue the process until you reach the point where the cost of mailing fund raising letters or the effort required to make calls isn't practical given the probable degree of success.

3. Figure out the best way (or ways) to solicit funds from the individuals you've identified—letters, door-to-door calls, telephone calls, benefits, other fund raising events, special calls on high-income people, establishing a "membership" program, and so on.

4. Try out your approach with a small group before you invest a lot of your time, the time of your board and other volunteers, and money.

5. If the results of your test or the full-fledged effort are disappointing, talk to some prospects to figure out why.

6. Don't overlook acknowledging individuals' contributions and keeping them informed of your activities, so they'll be primed to renew their contributions next time you ask. If you are able to secure large, noncash contributions, such as shares of stock, federal tax law (as of this revised edition) requires that taxpayers donating such gifts worth $250 or more obtain written acknowledgment that states whether or not any goods or services were provided in return for the gifts and, if so, their value.

Some Final Words

You and your dedicated volunteers can become adept at fund raising, but you must invest some time in studying how others are successful at it and then devise a strategy that best fits your organization's mission, capabilities, opportunities, needs, and so on. Read some books. If you're near one of the Foundation Centers, visit and study the myriad materials available. Attend a seminar devoted to fund raising basics and then go on to one that covers raising money from individuals (if that will be among your strategies), grant proposal writing (if you will be approaching foundations or corporations), benefit events (if that's in the cards for you), and so on.

Don't forget that when you have successfully raised some money, you must have in place the proper procedures to process and record the funds received and to produce reports in accordance with established financial standards (see the chapter on accounting).

Human Resources: Building Your Organization's Team

At this point you may be the only paid staff of your nonprofit organization, but even if this is so, don't skip over this chapter. You may lean heavily on volunteers to do what a paid staff does in a larger nonprofit, and whether your staff is paid or consists of unpaid volunteers, there are common principles involved in building a team and motivating people.

To a large extent, the identity of your program in the community and with your clients is determined by your staff—the employees and your volunteers. The community looks at your staff and sees your agency. A good program plan, a healthy budget, and a committed board cannot carry the ball without a qualified and motivated staff. Personnel issues for the new program include determining staffing needs, developing job descriptions (again, for all positions, whether paid or volunteer), recruiting people, and developing personnel policies.

What Kind of Staff Do You Need?

It is important to take the time and energy to consider carefully the staffing needs of your organization. In structuring your staff, it is more useful to work from the tasks to be performed to the kind of people needed than to name positions arbitrarily and then assign responsibilities to them. For instance, the program plan developed for your organization should specify in writing the goals and objectives of your program and the tasks necessary to reach those objectives. You can use this outline of tasks to determine the staffing pattern required to carry out the planned program.

1. Determine the skills needed for each task. The tasks (or functions or responsibilities, if you prefer those terms) should be

clustered by skill areas, such as administration, clerical support, counseling, education, lobbying, community relations, and fund raising.

2. Determine the length of time required to complete each task or function. How often must this activity be carried out? Daily, weekly, monthly, annually? How much time will it require?

3. Based on these skill groupings and time estimates, develop a list of the staff positions necessary to complete your planned tasks. For each position, the task assignments to be completed should be listed.

4. Consider the various staffing patterns available to your organization. There are many possible options besides having full-time paid staff positions. Alternatives include part-time paid positions, temporary paid staff, paid consultants, volunteers, college interns, and high school students. Creative use of staffing options can trim your budget and provide an energetic and skilled workforce that might otherwise be unavailable to community programs. Play around with various combinations of these options to determine which is most workable for your organization. The result should be a list of staff positions and task assignments, with specifications as to the type of employee (full- or part-time, regular or temporary, paid or voluntary, and so on) needed to fill each position.

5. Determine the salary ranges for each of the paid positions. By contacting other nonprofit agencies with similar staff positions, you can find out what salaries they are paying. Salary ranges (e.g., $15,000–$17,000 instead of $16,000) allow you to use some discretion when hiring staff, so that you can pay each individual according to his or her relevant education and experience.

6. Review your list of positions to determine whether such a staffing pattern would realistically allow for completion of the activities outlined in the program plan. Is the staffing pattern realistic in terms of the projected budget? Can you attract persons who have the needed skills with the proposed salaries? At this point, it may be necessary to revise the program plan to meet staff and budget limitations, to expand the budget to allow for a staff adequate to carry out the program

plan, or to readjust the staffing pattern to provide the skills you need without depending on a large and costly staff of full-time paid employees.

7. After completing the staff list, develop an organizational chart clarifying the decision-making process and the chain of command within your organization. The chart should diagram supervisory relationships among the staff and outline proposed reporting and communicating patterns. This will allow you to picture where in the organization each position fits. It will also help you determine the levels of responsibility of the staff members and the supervisory and administrative skills required in each position. It also will allow you to see how the staff members will work together as a team.

Organizational Models

There are a range of models that an organization can follow. On one end of the continuum is a loosely structured team in which all members have equal roles. The entire organization may operate as a team (whole group model) or there may be several teams. There may be no traditional supervisor, leader, or coordinator; instead, such roles are rotated among some or all members of the team. At the other end of the continuum is the traditional hierarchical structure under a manager with broad powers. Some organizational models combine features of both kinds of approaches. A fledgling organization can choose an organizational structure and then refine it or change to another model as the organization develops and grows.

Whole Group Model

Especially in small agencies, the whole group can operate as a team for many functions. Emphasis is on group decision making. Theoretically, if everyone is equally committed, self-motivated, and otherwise capable of team cooperation, a team leader is not necessary. However, in practice, any group generally needs someone to schedule meetings, to lead group members so that they're productive and everyone gets an opportunity to contribute, and to perform the other tasks of a process manager.

Hierarchical Model

The traditional hierarchical organizational structure consists of a manager/supervisor with people accountable to him or her for getting things done. Decisions are generally made by the supervisor with input and feedback from those supervised, but some decisions are delegated.

Team Model

In larger agencies, the staff can be broken into subgroups, such as by program or by major organizational functions. Each team functions similarly to that in the whole group model. The executive director or other senior manager coordinates the various teams.

Combination

An agency may choose to combine features of the above three organizational models to allow both group interaction and individual feedback and appraisal.

Job Descriptions: Putting It All Together

Job descriptions specifically define staff positions, outlining the major responsibilities of each position, its major task and function, and the background necessary to fulfill the responsibility the job entails. Job descriptions should be developed for each staff position, including volunteer and intern positions. Job descriptions are useful to the organization in several ways:

1. Developing them forces you to explain each position in objective, measurable terms.
2. They provide clear, standard descriptions of staff positions for potential applicants.
3. They serve as a basis for the development of screening and selection processes for applicants.
4. They provide guidelines for job performance and employee evaluation.

Although there are a variety of useful formats for job descriptions, most include three basic parts: the job's primary responsibilities and essential functions, any other activities the job may entail, and the level of education and experience that the job requires.

Primary Responsibilities

Generally, a one- to three-sentence statement explains the general areas of responsibility and gives a fairly broad description of the position. This statement should answer the question, What is the primary reason this position exists?

Essential Job Functions

The next section of the job description usually outlines in fairly specific terms the tasks and functions that are *essential* to the job. It's important that what is included here be truly central to the job. One useful format lists each major responsibility as a distinct, one-sentence statement and then outlines the major corresponding tasks for each. The tasks outlined under each single responsibility area are a response to the question, What would I actually have to do to fulfill this responsibility?

Other Activities

If there are other activities that the job holder will be asked to perform if possible, but that are not essential to fulfilling the requirements of the job, these could be listed here.

Educational and Experience Requirements

After you know what the person is responsible for and what major tasks the holder of a given position must perform, the next question is, What must a person know, or what skills and abilities must he or she have, in order to do those tasks? You should keep asking this question: If the applicants don't have a particular knowledge or skill, might they still be able to do the job while acquiring that knowledge and skill?

Sample Job Description

Job Title: Youth Counselor   *Reports to:* Executive Director
Supervises: Counseling Intern   *Date of This Description:* 11/1/95

Primary Responsibilities:

1. Provides individual and group treatment for youths in the program.
2. Develops individual treatment plans for youths in caseload.

Essential Job Functions (For each function, you may wish to estimate the percentage of time most likely expended on these activities, possibly using a range of time per function. This can later be used in determining the extent to which the job holder is meeting the critical requirements of the job. However, some jobs may not be readily broken down by percentage of time for each activity because this varies so much from week to week.)

A. Provide individual counseling for six to eight youths at least once a week, developing treatment plan with the youths, setting up monthly behavioral contracts with them, and assessing their needs. 20–30%

B. Facilitate daily group sessions with youths. 20–30%

C. Maintain relationships with families, schools, and court workers of youths and with related community agencies. 10–20%

D. Facilitate family sessions for those who request it. 10–20%

E. Develop volunteer service placements for young clients. 10%

Other Activities:

A. As time permits, serves as a member of the program counseling developmental team and attends staff meetings.

B. Works with other youth counselors in mentoring and supervising interns.

Requirements:

1. *Skills and knowledge:* demonstrated knowledge of group and individual counseling skills, a working knowledge of community youth resources, ability to work with youths and their families, behavior planning skills.

2. *Education:* training in individual, group, and family counseling.

3. *Experience:* at least three years' experience in youth work.

Desired but not required skills, education, experience:

1. B.A. degree in psychology, sociology, or related field.

2. Skill in planning and implementing recreational activities.

3. Awareness of alternative educational systems, court services, drugs and their effects, symptoms of learning disabilities.

4. Experience in youth outreach work.

Be aware that loading everything you'd like to have into the "requirements" of the job, versus what is truly essential, could lead to difficulty in recruiting a qualified person for the salary available or may unfairly eliminate people who would make a significant contribution to your mission. Job requirements should be stated in terms of the specific skills needed. Other knowledge and experience that would be helpful in the position can be listed as "desired" rather than "required." This additional information can help applicants understand more about the job, but care should be taken to ensure that the position is not restricted to those who also have skills and knowledge listed as "desired."

Help Wanted: Recruiting and Screening Candidates

Once the necessary positions have been identified and the preliminary job descriptions written, you can begin making decisions about how to recruit people for paid and volunteer positions, what procedures to use in screening résumés and applications, how you are going to select your final candidate(s), who you want involved in each of these steps, and when the steps should be taken.

Generally, the best way to attract qualified staff people is to use as many advertising media as possible, but this can get expensive. The most commonly used resources are local newspapers, especially the Sunday editions, which reach masses of people, but don't overlook the publications serving communities of color. Neighborhood and other weekly papers may also be useful, especially in recruiting volunteers if your program is focused on a particular geographic area. You could also send your job notices to special interest publications in your field, professional newsletters and journals, related agencies, and placement offices at colleges and universities. Ask people at other nonprofits if there is a local central registry of nonprofit staff positions available and a placement facility for volunteers. You may also find interns through college and university departments.

Employment ads should include the job's title, a brief description of the job's responsibilities and functions, a list of the required skills and background, the employing agency and its address, the materials required for application, and the deadline for submitting those materials. This information can be summarized from the basic job description you compiled during the planning stages.

Consider whether you want to require written résumés or applications. On the one hand, you can use résumés or written applications to screen out applicants who clearly appear unqualified for the position, rather than doing this in personal interviews or over the telephone. On the other hand, the best information about someone's qualifications for the job usually comes from the applicant, and not all applicants express themselves well in written material. By depending solely on written material for prescreening applicants, you may discriminate against qualified applicants who have not presented themselves well on paper. Whichever way you go, it is important to be consistent. If you choose written résumés as the method for prescreening applicants (most hiring in social service agencies is done this way), be sure to examine all of the résumés carefully, looking for the basic skills you require.

You also must be aware of what information you can legally request in applications and in interviews. Some information you should not ask on applications or interviews can be obtained after a person has been employed. The rules vary by state, so you should call whatever state agency handles human rights to find out your legal limitations.

Reviewing Résumés

You must develop a simple but fair procedure for reviewing résumés and judging each applicant's potential for doing the job. This process is necessarily subjective, but the aim is to be as objective as possible. You must be able to get beyond simply saying, "I think

I like this person better than that person," and be able to justify that preference based on your actual hiring criteria.

One review method is based on a two-step process: (1) selecting those who indicate that they have the minimum skills required for the job and (2) judging the skill levels of those with at least minimal skills. A written rating scale can be developed for reviewing résumés during these two steps. The knowledge, skills, and experience outlined in the job description are used as criteria for the résumé review tool.

Skill rating based on résumés is not an exact, perfectly reliable science. It is simply an effort to be more precise than totally subjective, off-the-cuff judgments allow you to be. Keep this shortcoming in mind when designing and using a résumé review tool. Your rating scale should be defined in simple, clear terms so that all involved in the review process have a common understanding of the criteria. The skills and knowledge you require should be translated into measurable terms, when possible.

Each item can be assigned a rating scale, either a two-step (has/does not have minimum capacity) or a three- to five-level scale based on the applicant's number of years' experience, level of responsibility, skills, and so on. Each item should indicate the minimum level of skill or experience acceptable. If an applicant does not indicate at least minimal skills on all items, he or she would not be considered further.

When using the scale, you should not be so restrictive as to eliminate applicants unfairly because they do not have exactly the right kind of experience; people can learn skills through many types of experience, and their capabilities may not be represented on paper exactly as you expect them to be.

During the initial review step, you should reject only those applicants deemed unqualified. The next step is to judge the quality and quantity of the skills of those applicants who pass the initial review. As a result of this step, you will develop a small pool of applicants to interview (perhaps five to ten).

Before interviewing the final applicants, jot down notes on areas in which you need more specific information based on their résumés. You can use these to formulate questions for the interview.

Interviewing

In most situations you can judge the basic skills of applicants through their résumés, but a further step is needed to choose among those who seem to have the ability to do the job. The interview can elicit much more information than it is possible to get from a résumé. It gives both the employer and the applicant a chance to ask questions that have developed during earlier stages of the hiring process. However, the flexibility and subjectivity of interviewing make it a double-edged tool. It has the potential of supplying crucial information for decisions, but it also has equal potential for unfairly screening out qualified candidates.

Standardized interviews can be designed to allow you to treat applicants equally and compare different people. If you do not have parallel information on different applicants, comparison will be very difficult. Interviews for all applicants can be structured so that they closely resemble each other in content and format. Write down the questions you wish to have answered and ask them of all applicants, use the same interviewers, and develop a means of noting answers and rating them.

Loosely structured interviews rely on questions tailored to each individual applicant. This allows you to round out the information contained in the résumés. It is often helpful to hear applicants explain their experience and skills. This also allows you to determine more specifically the strengths and weaknesses of each applicant and to draw more individual images of each person you interview.

Interviews can be designed to balance standardization with flexibility. Several open-ended questions can be developed that are appropriate for all applicants and allow you to compare responses. Other questions can be developed specifically for each person to be interviewed. Most interview questions should be open-ended. If possible, several people should interview candidates and a combination of the interviewers' conclusions can be used as the basis of the selection.

You may wish to narrow the choice down to two or three candidates after the first interview and then interview these final candidates a second time. During the second interview, you may wish to involve other staff members who will be working with this person. Since you have already discussed the quality of these candidates, the second interview can focus on related values and attitudes, work style, and preferences regarding management and supervision.

Hiring

After the candidates have been interviewed, but before you make your final selection, contact the people listed as references by the final candidates. Ask the references to confirm the reliability of the individuals and the quality of their past work. However, you may find that the references will not go beyond confirming that the candidate was employed in a particular position and the dates of employment. Many employers, particularly larger organizations, have policies that prevent supervisors from making any comment on the performance or other qualities of former employees, because of the fear of lawsuits. Nevertheless, contacting references is still a way to determine whether applicants have presented themselves accurately on paper and in person.

When the final selection has been made, the individual chosen should be formally offered the job. A written offer to hire should include a brief summary of the job's responsibilities, the starting salary and fringe benefits provided, the beginning date of work, the number of work hours expected of a part-time employee (if appropriate), any special agreements or arrangements between the agency and the new employee, the signature of the executive director, and a copy of the agency's personnel policies.

As soon as a candidate has accepted the position, all those who applied for the job should be notified as quickly as possible that the position has been filled.

Fair Employment Practices

There are certain restrictions on your freedom to hire, promote, pay, and fire people under federal law, state laws, and, often, a city's human rights statutes. Violating those restrictions, even unwittingly, could subject your organization (and you) to a lawsuit or other difficulties. This is a minefield, and you'd better equip yourself with a map. As suggested earlier, you should call the agencies of your state and city that are responsible for human rights. They will be able to provide you with appropriate material specifying your legal responsibilities. Also, local educational organizations or associations may offer courses on legal employment practices. But beyond the legalities, a responsible organization will want to treat people of various human characteristics fairly and with dignity.

Caution must be taken to protect the rights of applicants during all phases of hiring. As a prospective employer, you must be careful not to place unjust or unsupportable demands on applicants. Be careful to demand the knowledge, skills, abilities, and experience that you are confident are necessary for effective job performance. You should be continually asking yourself, Why do I want this information? Does the answer really have a bearing on the person's ability to do the job? If you are ever questioned about why you chose certain selection procedures, you will be responsible for proving their validity.

The following areas should never be included as questions on applications, in résumé reviews, or in interviews: age, race, gender, marital status, number and age of children, child-care arrangements, weekend work capacity (unless part of regular work), credit records, public assistance status, medical history, workers' compensation history, arrest and conviction records, and disabilities.

"Valuing diversity" or "creating a pluralistic organization" has increasingly become a focus of all types of employers. Many businesses, educational institutions, government agencies, and nonprofits have adopted statements along these lines:

> We will not discriminate against or harass any employee or applicant for employment because of race, color, creed, religion, national origin, ancestry, gender, sexual orientation, age, disability, marital status, or status with regard to public assistance. We take affirmative action to ensure that employment practices are free of such discrimination. We realize that some groups are underrepresented in employment.

We affirm the value of human diversity and seek to manage all aspects of our organization so that every individual has the opportunity to achieve his or her fullest potential regardless of any particular human characteristic.

As a new and most likely small-staffed organization, you probably won't be subject to the American with Disabilities Act, which currently applies to employers with fifteen or more paid employees. However, its provisions reflect the responsible treatment of people with disabilities, and some state and local laws may apply similar provisions to all organizations. Under the ADA, an employer must make "reasonable accommodations" to the known disability of an otherwise qualified employee or applicant, unless the employer can show that the accommodation will impose undue hardship.

If you have problems trying to design fair employment procedures, contact your state department of human rights or the personnel department of larger cities or counties for guidelines.

Carefully document all aspects of your recruitment and hiring practices as a safeguard against allegations of discrimination. The dates and texts of ads and the publications in which the ads were placed should be recorded, and the hiring procedures should be outlined in writing.

Personnel Policies

Personnel policies are written guidelines defining the relationship between an agency and its staff. They spell out what the agency expects of the staff, what the staff can expect from the agency, and what the procedures are for resolving work-related conflicts. Well-written policies can promote good communication between your agency and its employees, and can prevent conflicts arising from misunderstandings.

Your board of directors should hold itself accountable for the existence of written personnel policies. You may want to seek the help of a director or a special ad hoc committee of the board to draft the policies. Ideally, personnel policies should be determined during an early stage of the agency's development. The input of the director of the agency, and of any other staff members who have already been hired, aids the development of workable, satisfactory policies. Ask organizations similar to yours that have reputations for being well managed for copies of their policies to use as models. Your own personnel policies, however, should be tailored to fit your organization's needs and values.

The personnel policies should be formally accepted by the board of directors They should be reviewed from time to time and revised, when necessary, to reflect new organizational needs and capacities. Each employee should be given a copy of the policies.

The following outline can be followed in developing personnel policies.

Personnel Policy Guidelines

Introduction: Briefly describe the process used for developing the policies, including the date of approval and the recommended period for reviews of policies. Caution: In some states, court decisions have ruled that the contents of written policies create employment contracts that may be difficult to revise as conditions change. Thus, you may need to include a "disclaimer" such as the following: *The policies, procedures, definitions, and other material are in effect at the sole discretion of management and may be revised or withdrawn at any time without notice. This material is not intended nor shall it be construed as a binding contract.*

Employee Definitions: Define full-time employee, part-time employee (in terms of numbers of hours worked; you may use a range of hours), temporary employee, volunteer employee, and any other classification of employee to be used by your agency. Eligibility for benefits should be defined.

Hiring Practices: Hiring procedures and policies, including advertisement, screening, selection, and promotion considerations, should be explained. A statement explaining affirmative action and equal employment policies should be included also. (Check to see which federal and state laws apply to your agency because of its size, nature, and funding sources.)

Employee Evaluations: Explain employee evaluation procedures, including periodic performance reviews.

Termination Procedures: Practices regarding voluntary termination, involuntary termination, and reductions in workforce, including notification regarding termination, should be specified. Appeal procedures available to employees should be outlined.

Salaries: Agency policy regarding salary schedules, salary reviews, and reimbursement for travel, overtime, use of personal car for agency business, and other expenses should be specified, as should the schedule for paydays.

Benefits (if any): Explain any health and life insurance coverages provided to employees. Any staff development or training benefits should also be described, including funds or leaves available to employees for education or training.

Absences, Vacations, and Holidays: Specify paid or unpaid time away from work that is available to employees and rate of accumulation, procedures for arranging time off, eligibility restrictions, and salary policies for each of the following: vacation, sick leave, holidays, personal days, leaves of absence, maternity/paternity leaves, and jury duty.

Hours: The minimum hours of work required per week, the daily office or program hours, and procedures for variances from these should be specified. Large employers in particular are likely to have all this written out in plain English for their supervisors, so see if you can get a copy, or call your state's department of labor and industry (or equivalent department).

Personnel Files: Explain the contents of personnel files, procedures for access, and the procedures for challenging or adding to the materials included in them.

Performance Management

Even if you have only one, part-time employee reporting to you, good performance management is the best way to produce results for your organization. And much of what applies to employee performance management can be transferred to getting the most from volunteers.

Some people do not perform as well as their education, experience, talents, and so on indicate they should. Their performance may be "minimally satisfactory" in terms of what is expected, but only that. When this is the case, most likely they're responding to their total working environment. An organization can have wonderful statements of mission, vision, values, and so on, but those alone do not create a motivating working climate. Good performance management includes the following:

1. Clear communication of the mission and vision of the organization, how the employee's work fits in with the mission and vision, and what is expected of the employee.
2. Managers' asking for and listening to employees' suggestions for getting the work done well.
3. Reinforcement of good behavior and performance. (This won't work if you feel you must also recite deficiencies in some other aspect of the employee's work. There's a time and place for that, but not when you're trying to reinforce positive performance.)
4. At a minimum, an annual performance appraisal for each employee, at which time you review, for the whole job, the ways in which the employee is doing well and any improvement opportunities. Many experienced supervisors find it useful to ask the employee to do a self-appraisal first. This allows you to consider what, if any, gaps exist between the employee's perception of his or her job performance and yours so that you can better prepare for a productive discussion.

Community Relations: Staying in Touch

The relations you develop with your community are crucial to the success of your program. Who is your community? It consists, first of all, of those your program was designed to serve. Depending upon your program, your client constituency may be disadvantaged people who need the services you offer, all residents of a neighborhood, other individuals, nonprofit organizations, or some other group. But there likely are others as well whose understanding and support of what you're all about are important to your organization. These could include community leaders, government agencies with an interest in the population you serve, potential donors, and state and local elected officials. These various segments of the community are your "publics."

Within some nonprofit organizations, the process of developing effective relations with various publics is known as *marketing, public affairs*, or *public relations*. Regardless of the label, we're talking about a management process that analyzes and interprets the knowledge and perspectives of your organization's various publics that could affect the organization positively or negatively; that informs those publics of the organization's goals, activities, and policies; and that attempts to influence public opinion and public policy so that it is favorable toward the organization and its mission. Related activities include media relations, advertising, newsletters and brochures, membership recruitment, special events, public meetings, and personal interaction of staff and board members with those in the community. Good relations with your publics can attract clients, members, volunteers, or other participants; help secure financial resources; and provide useful input in converting these resources into programs and services.

Nonprofit groups, as well as businesses, engage in public, or community, relations. Every organized group is involved in community relations—whether it knows it or not and whether it has planned for it or not. And these relations are having an impact on the

116   Community Relations

program—for better or, sometimes, for worse. Unless you develop community relations according to a well-thought-out plan, your efforts in this area will have limited, transitory, and perhaps harmful effects.

Developing a plan for effective community relations will help an organization to achieve its program's objectives. The success of a program depends as much on the people outside of the agency as it does on those within. The support of your community—of clients, members, other agencies and professionals, funders, community residents and leaders—is essential.

Planning effective community relations involves the following steps:

1. Defining your community—your publics
2. Determining the objectives of your community relations
3. Deciding the messages to be conveyed to your community
4. Selecting the media for communication with your community
5. Outlining and carrying out your community relations plan
6. Evaluating the results

Who should be involved in developing your community relations plan? The input of both board and staff is essential. It works best when one person is designated to be responsible for overseeing the community relations of your organization. If the staff is large enough and has some expertise in this area, a staff member can perform this role. In many cases, a board member serves as public relations chair, perhaps working with a committee. You may be able to recruit someone with experience in this area to serve as a board member in this role. One option is to have a public relations chair on the board who works closely with one staff person—perhaps the executive director, assistant director, or information coordinator—to develop and administer community relations plans. In any case, the input of other board and staff members is important; they can bring additional insight and expertise to this planning process, and their support will be needed to carry out your public relations plans.

The following community relations planning guide is supplemented by worksheets at the end of this chapter.

Step 1: Define Your Community (Worksheet A)

The first step in community relations planning is to identify those groups with whom your organization has, or should have, relationships. These groups are your publics. You probably do not have one broad, homogeneous public; rather, you likely have many smaller, identifiable groups. These groups vary according to the nature of the organization. A community theater establishes relationships with theatergoers, actors, and others involved in producing plays and funders interested in the arts. A youth group may want to reach youths, their parents, school officials, and other youth agencies in the area.

Some of publics may be organized—other agencies, service clubs, other special interest associations, political parties, neighborhood associations, government bodies. Some are not organized but are easily identified—members, clients, families of clients, funders, and certain community leaders. Other groups are larger, unorganized, and less easily identified—senior citizens, music lovers, smokers, potentially delinquent youths, and businesspeople.

In order to identify your publics, ask yourself: To whom will you be providing services? Who do you want to attract to your program? Will you be referring clients to anyone else? Will you be receiving clients referred from other sources? Who will be providing funding and other support for the program? Are there groups you will be trying to influence? Who will be trying to influence you? Are there those whose goodwill you depend on? The answers to these questions should provide you with an outline of the major groups in the community with whom you have or will be establishing relationships.

Each of these major groups, or markets, should then be divided into smaller units, or segments. This segmentation will allow you to examine the differences among each of these groups based on their interests, needs, perceptions, size, and so on. Your community relations plan should take into account these differences among the segments of your market in order to be more effective in reaching all of the segments. Each may require a different message sent through different media and aimed at different objectives. You may want different things from each of your publics.

It can be helpful to rate the relative importance of each of these segments to your organization in order to set priorities for your efforts and avoid spending a lot of time and effort reaching groups that are relatively unimportant to you while ignoring more significant groups. *Importance* can be defined in terms of the extent to which a group can have an impact on your program or the extent to which you feel your program can have an impact on the group.

Step 2: Determine the Objectives of Your Community Relations Plan (Worksheet B)

What do you want your community relations plan to accomplish? In broad terms, you want your community to support you and to use your resources appropriately. But the objectives of your plan must be more specific. What kinds of community support do you need in order to achieve your program? In many cases, your public relations objectives may parallel your program objectives. As with program objectives, public relations objectives must be specific, realistic, and measurable in terms of numbers of people, dates, money, and so on. They should be concerned with results rather than process. In addition, they should be agreed upon and written down. Revisit your strategic plan to see what community relations objectives are needed to support your mission, vision, and strategic goals.

Objectives can be short-term, related to a specific community relations effort, or ongoing, aimed at maintaining a certain level of performance. What do you want your public to think or do as a result of your communication with them? This should be something very specific, such as becoming a participant in your program, referring others to your program, providing funding, establishing a service contract with you, supporting your presence in the community, or attending a concert. You may also want a response that is more difficult to perceive: for example, a change in attitude toward your program or an increase in the level of knowledge about a particular issue. In either case, you should be able to pinpoint the intended response closely enough that you will later be able to tell whether your communication succeeded. The following are some examples of possible objectives:

1. To attract thirty new inquiries from potential volunteers each month from September through December.
2. To increase by 10 percent the number of clients referred by the community's high schools during the following school year.
3. To achieve newspaper reviews of all theatrical productions (presumably, achieving favorable reviews will depend on the quality of the performances and not on your public relations effort!).
4. To develop a service contract with the county by January.
5. To create a positive attitude among the majority of neighborhood residents toward our facility.
6. To maintain theater attendance at the current level for the next season.

Step 3: Decide the Messages to be Conveyed (Worksheet C)

What information do you wish to convey to each of the publics you have identified? What impression do you want them to have of your program? What idea do you want to get across? What are you offering to the community? If you have done an adequate job of program planning, this step will be just about complete. You should have already assessed the needs of the community you will be serving. You should have defined those particular needs that your program will be addressing. And you should have a clear description of the programs and services to be provided.

Use this information to arrive at a description of the program or, in a sense, the "product" that you are offering to the community. Briefly outline each service your organization provides and the need for each service. Emphasize each service's uniqueness. What are the characteristics of the service that will appeal to the community you wish to serve? Such features may be related to its availability elsewhere in the community, the background of the staff, the program, its philosophy, its target constituency, its price, and the uniqueness of the program. In other words, what should you *stress* about your program when you tell the community about it? Why should the community care?

How do your publics regard you? What impression do they have of you? This image can be described in terms of expertise, confidence level, comfortability, and accessibility. Are you considered to be competent, trustworthy? Are your staff considered outsiders in the community? Do your publics know what you offer and at what cost, and how to get involved in your program?

If you are unsure of your image in the community, develop a feedback mechanism to give you this information. Formal feedback, through polls and surveys, can be costly, but you should be able to conduct small-scale surveys periodically. Questionnaires to be completed by current members or participants are relatively easy to develop and administer. However, most of your community feedback will probably be "anecdotal," gleaned through meetings, interviews, and casual discussions with members of your various publics. Even such anecdotal measures, if collected systematically and without filtering out unpleasant feedback, can tell you much about your program's image and provide good information to improve your program.

In turn, how do you want each of your markets to regard you? What impression of you do you wish them to have? Are there any discrepancies between what people see in your organization and what you want them to see? If so, how can these be minimized? The results of this exercise are important to consider when you are designing your message to the community. You must take care to establish an identity that you feel truly represents you and design communications that reinforce this image. In some cases, you may have to make some program changes in order to develop a more positive image in the community.

At this point, you should have a good idea of the messages you wish to convey, and you can write your messages out briefly and simply. For example:

1. Forming block clubs will reduce crime in your neighborhood.
2. Buying a season theater ticket saves you money and time.

3. Your financial support will send 50 disadvantaged children to camp.

4. We are an effective and qualified program to which you can refer troubled youths.

Such statements will be the basis for your communications with your publics.

Step 4: Select the Media (Worksheet D)

The communications media to be considered include television and radio spots, newspaper ads and articles, posters, videotapes, brochures, newsletters, booths, speaking engagements, personal meetings, special events, billboards, and door-to-door campaigns. In recent years, on-line services such as CompuServe, Prodigy, and America Online, which provide access to the Internet, local electronic bulletin boards, community "freenets," and more, have offered increased communications opportunities to nonprofits.

Generally, you should use more than one type of communication to convey your message. The media available offer a range of possibilities and vary in the amount of money and expertise they require. The second part of Worksheet D, at the end of this chapter, describes the pros and cons of various media. Certain media may be more effective than others for reaching particular audiences.

Where can you reach your publics? Are they generally at home, in school, at work, in clubs, involved with the courts or other agencies? This information provides a key to choosing the most appropriate medium for reaching your audience.

What else do they do? The answer to this question is often helpful when you are choosing a main medium or a secondary channel of communication. What kinds of activities do they participate in? Watching television, listening to the radio, attending church or other social activities, participating in clubs or cultural activities, going to a doctor? You should try to reach your audience by using the channels they already use.

When selecting media, ask yourself: Will this medium help us achieve our goals? Will it reach our target audience? Can we do a good job with this medium? Can someone help us use it more effectively? How much will it cost? Can we afford it? Are the projected results worth the cost?

Step 5: Finalize Community Relations Plan (Worksheet E)

The next step is to consolidate your community relations planning steps into a workable plan that includes target dates and who will do what. As a result of the last exercise, you should have considered possible channels of communication, the costs and resources required by each, their potential impacts, and any drawbacks they may have for your organization (such as relatively high cost). Draw on the resources of your board members to help make decisions regarding the most appropriate media for your purposes. If none of your board members has expertise in this area, chances are that someone on the board can refer you to others with that knowledge.

Once you have made these decisions, outline the specific activities that correspond to each of the community relations objectives you have already identified. Examples of such activities include the following:

1. Design and distribute five hundred brochures on our agency to potential referral sources.
2. Prepare a news release regarding the organization's stand on proposed legislation and distribute it to local daily and community newspapers.
3. Design a booth and arrange for participation in a state conference.
4. Conduct personal meetings with staff at twelve agencies and schools that are potential referral sources.
5. Develop a radio spot explaining the hot line aimed at youths and place it for airing on youth-oriented stations.

Outline your community relations plan in terms of the resources necessary: people, time, materials, and money. Be realistic. What can your agency afford? You should consider community relations costs when you plan your budget. Community relations is not a frivolous extra; you need to plan on spending time and money on it, because it can be crucial to the success of your organization.

For each activity, pinpoint the date, at least by month, by which the activity should be complete. Identify the staff member or volunteer who will complete the activity or take responsibility for its completion. Any needed resources should be identified: equipment, facilities, information, skills outside of your agency. Determine the cost of completing this activity. Such expenses may include production or printing costs, paper, postage, computerized mailing lists, and consulting or design fees. You may also wish to determine how much the activity will cost in terms of staff time, converted to a dollar figure, when possible.

The list of resources, skills, and expenses may seem overwhelming initially, but consider all of the resources in your community on which you can draw for help: public relations, advertising, and graphic arts departments of the businesses and corporations that fund you, that your board members work for, or that may be interested in providing such a donation can provide design, production, and printing assistance. Public relations and advertising agencies may be willing to "adopt" your agency for a period as a public service. Professional associations of journalists and other communication professionals may help you locate volunteers. Schools of journalism and/or advertising at local colleges and universities may be interested in helping you. A media resource center for nonprofit agencies may be available, if you are in a large metropolitan area.

Step 6: Evaluate Your Efforts (Worksheet F)

After you have carried out your planned activities, it is important to determine what you have accomplished. For each activity, determine how you will evaluate its success. What questions can be asked that, when answered, will tell you whether the community relations objective has been met? You may have to set up an information or record-keeping system that will allow you to answer these questions. For example:

1. How many callers heard about you through the radio spot? (You will have to ask them when they call.)
2. How many clients were referred by the agencies you met with? (You will have to record this information.)
3. How many of the local media carried articles based on your news release? (Monitor and keep clips of those that were used.)

If you received outside assistance in designing your communication, you can approach your volunteers or consultants again after the results are in to help you determine what went right or wrong, how future results could be improved, and how to follow up on this communication.

After you have carried out one community relations program and evaluated its effectiveness, you will be able to develop the next phase in your effort to communicate with your public. Community relations must be an ongoing process of listening to the concerns of your identified community, telling them what you have to say about your issue or your program, and listening again for their response.

Take It a Bit at a Time

To the novice in the field of community relations, the plan just described probably seems overwhelming. Your initial list of the various groups that make up your community and the subgroups within them will probably seem enormous and out of your control. It is! The utility of this planning guide is that it can help you identify potential community relations activities. From the endless agenda of things you could be doing to interact with the various groups in your community, you must choose which are the highest priority, most feasible, most affordable in terms of time as well as money, and most likely to get results.

Begin with a limited plan and choose a few activities that you feel you can do well. When these are completed, review what you have done. How did it go? What could you have done better? What did you do well? Did you get some results? Where do you go from here?

Worksheet A
Determine Who You Want to Reach

Publics: With whom should you interact?	Public Segments: Who are specific target groups?	Relative Importance (1 = high, 5 = low)
Funders	1. Foundations 2. Businesses 3. Government 4. Individual donors	• • • •
Volunteers	1. From businesses 2. Neighborhood 3. 4.	• • • •
Clientele	1. 2. 3.	• • •
Public opinion makers	1. Media editorialists 2. Political reporters 3. Other reporters 4. Public officials 5.	• • • • •
Church leaders	1. 2.	• •

Worksheet B
Determine Your Objectives

Objective	Target Date or Time Span
1.	
2.	
3.	
4.	
5.	
6.	

Worksheet C
Determine Your Message(s)

Public Segment	The Information: What do you want them to know or do?	The Message: What should you tell them?
1.		
2.		
3.		
4.		
5.		
6.		

Worksheet D
Selecting the Media

Part I: Pros and Cons of Various Media

Medium	Pros	Cons	Most Effective Use
Personal contacts	• Trust more easily established • Immediate feedback possible • Greatest impact	• Time-consuming • Impractical for large public • "Getting in" may be difficult	• Introduce self or program to key people
Brochure	• Control of message • Low-cost pieces can be effective • Mass mailings can be targeted to individuals	• Competes with many other items • Recipients may not absorb key messages • Difficult to secure immediate feedback	• Mailing list is up-to-date with right individuals • Easy to read • Designed for both skim and detailed reading
Poster, billboard	• Control message • Can reach large group or target narrow audience • Usually easy to deliver	• Competes with many other items • Short message • Generally no immediate feedback • Can be expensive	• Short, quickly absorbed message • High-impact message
Print advertising	• Control message • Easy to deliver • Detailed messages possible • Can reach large audience	• Competes with many other ads • Ads in daily newspapers and magazines generally expensive	• Need quick delivery • Seeking response • Detailed message
Radio advertising	• Control message • May secure free public service announcement (long shot) • Stations have defined audiences • Can have high impact	• No visual image • Need quality taped message • Expensive • Generally no immediate feedback • Message must be short	• For high impact • Simple message • Able to use listeners' imaginations for images • Refer listeners to sources—"look us up in phone book"
TV advertising	• Same as radio but also provides visual images	• Need quality production • Expensive • Generally no immediate feedback • Message must be short	• For high impact • Simple message • Refer listeners to sources—"look us up in phone book"

Part I: Pros and Cons of Various Media

Medium	Pros	Cons	Most Effective Use
News releases	• Inexpensive • May reach broad audience or very focused public	• Publication can (usually will) edit news release • Strong competition for editors' attention • High impact difficult to achieve	• Simple announcements • Message will appeal to daily media • Want to reach people through weekly newspapers
Speech or slide show	• Potential for dramatic portrayal of your program • High impact • Can target public • Q&A opportunity • Longer message possible • Inexpensive	• Takes time to arrange and time to write speech • Requires effective public speaking • If sensitive topic, Q&A can be disastrous if not capably handled	• Need to reach small, key public • Need to reach opinion makers • Need high impact • Message is of high potential interest • Speakers are well trained, very capable
Videotapes	• Potential for dramatic portrayal of your program • High impact • Can target public • Longer message possible	• Expensive to produce and distribute • Requires equipment	• Classroom • Seminars • Message requires high-impact visuals • Supplement speech
Special events and booths	• Can achieve high impact with target audience • Can be low cost	• Can require considerable time of staff and/or volunteers	• High impact or interaction is critical
On-line services	• Well-educated and involved audience • Accommodates Q&A • Can post messages quickly	• Requires computer modem, software, knowledge • May involve fees for access • Postings must be noncommercial	• Quickly mobilize people with like interests

Part II: Determine the Media to Use

Public Segment	Options: How to Reach Them	Decision: What Media to Use
Foundations	1. Letters 2. Personal calls 3. Grant proposals 4. Brochures	

Worksheet E
Community Relations Plan

(Complete one worksheet for each objective.)

Objective No. _____:

Actions (Media etc.) to Achieve Objective	Date	Person Responsible	Expense	Measure of Success

Worksheet F
Evaluation of Results

(Complete one worksheet for each objective.)

Objective No. _____:

Activity	Measure	Results

Sources of Assistance: You're Not Alone

Many organizations can provide you with advice, information, and various services. Some of these come free, some involve relatively low fees, and some cost a bundle. The most expensive advice, information, and services are those that lead you down the wrong path or waste your time. Following are several suggested approaches for securing quality assistance.

1. State associations of nonprofit organizations exist in about half of the U.S. states. Membership fees vary. They offer a variety of products and services, such as technical assistance, educational programs, insurance plans, group purchasing programs, advocacy on public policy issues, and referrals to other sources of assistance. To determine if an association exists in your state and, if so, how to contact it, write or call the National Council of Nonprofit Associations, 1001 Connecticut Ave. NW, Suite 900, Washington, DC 20036; telephone (202) 833-5740; fax (202) 833-5747. The NCNA is the national coalition of state associations of nonprofits, representing more than twenty thousand community-based organizations whose purpose is to enhance the quality of life in their communities.

2. Quality educational programs designed for nonprofit practitioners and ranging from short workshops to multiple-session courses are available in many states. Some university schools of business offer courses tailored to the needs of nonprofit practitioners. "Academic centers" devoted to nonprofit management education and other services also exist in some states. Most are affiliated with universities. At the time of this writing, more than eighty business schools offered at least a few courses designed specifically for nonprofit practitioners. If you locate an association of nonprofit organizations in your state as suggested above, it should be able to tell you about various sources of nonprofit-oriented educational programs. Or call your state attorney general's office and ask to speak to who-

ever handles matters relating to charities; request referral to any local organization providing educational services.

3. Telecommunications services may be available from some local organizations serving nonprofits. The Telecommunications Cooperative Network serves all states. This nonprofit cooperative purchases, on behalf of its 3,500 members, long-distance phone service, conference calling, auditorium teleconferencing, 800/900 numbers, audiotext, fax broadcasting, fax on demand, and electronic data communications and other services and states that it achieves 10–20 percent savings. For information on membership and services, write TCN at 2101 Wilson Blvd., Suite 417, Arlington, VA 22201; fax (703) 243-0202.

4. The Foundation Center is a nonprofit organization organized and supported by foundations. It is an authoritative source of information on foundation giving. It produces directories describing specific foundations (their program interests and fiscal and personnel data), grants indexes (listings of recent grants by foundations), and publications on how to do funding research, proposal writing, and other fund raising activities. For example, you can find out what New York foundations support urban projects and get the names of their officers and trustees. Or you can get the names and addresses of smaller foundations in a certain zip code range. If you are fortunate enough to have on-line (electronic) retrieval capabilities, you can access the Center's computer. The Center's printed directories, and other Center publications, are available from the Center or by visiting one of the more than eighty libraries or other agencies around the country that are "affiliates" of the Foundation Center. To obtain the name of the library collection nearest you, call toll-free (800) 424-9836.

5. The Independent Sector is an organization that promotes effectiveness within the nonprofit sector, providing materials on leadership and management, data on giving trends, and other information. Prices of materials are discounted for IS members. Contact this organization at 1828 L Street NW, Washington, DC 20036; telephone (202) 223-8100.

6. The National Center for Nonprofit Boards is dedicated to improving the effectiveness of nonprofit organizations by strengthening their boards of directors. NCNB was created in 1988 by the Independent Sector and the Association of Governing Boards of Universities and Colleges. You can contact NCNB at 2000 L Street NW, Suite 411, Washington, DC 20036; telephone (202) 452-6262; fax (202) 452-6262.

7. The Nonprofit Management Association is a national network of organizations and individuals who are engaged in improving the management of nonprofits. Its membership includes management support organizations in a number of states, executive directors, independent consultants, academicians, and funders. Contact the association at 310 Madison Ave., Suite 1630, New York, NY 10017; telephone (212) 949-0990; fax (212) 949-1672.

8. Your local library and some university libraries may have collections of books on various nonprofit topics, including some of the books listed in the bibliography.

9. The Nonprofit Risk Management Center offers training, technical assistance, and publications on insurance, liability issues, and other risk reduction for nonprofits. For information, write to 1001 Connecticut Ave. NW, Suite 900, Washington, DC 20036; telephone (202) 785-3891.

Nonprofit Management Bibliography

Many books are available on nonprofit management and other nonprofit sector subjects. (One publisher, Jossey-Bass, produces a "nonprofit sector series" that includes a variety of useful books.) This bibliography lists some of the books and publications that should be especially useful to those engaged in starting a nonprofit organization. Some items are not available through bookstores, but must be ordered from the originating organizations (see end of bibliography for addresses).

Books Covering Multiple Management Subjects

A Nonprofit Organization Operating Manual: Planning for Survival and Growth. By Arnold J. Olenick and Phillip R. Olenick. New York: The Foundation Center, 1991. A guide to acquiring and managing sources crucial to the life of a nonprofit; covers incorporation, legal obligations, accounting methods (written for nonaccountants), budgeting strategies, tax returns, fund raising, organizational management, auditing policies, income-producing ventures, and long-range planning. 477 pages. Order from the Foundation Center.

Managing a Nonprofit Organization. By Thomas Wolf. New York: Prentice Hall Press, 1990. Provides concise guide to nonprofit management. Covers the selection of board members, financing, fund raising, staffing, computerizing, planning, and marketing. Includes illustrations and checklists to aid in understanding of management theory and practices. 296 pages.

Managing Nonprofit Organizations in the 21st Century. By James P. Gelatt. Phoenix: Oryx Press, 1992. Addresses emerging issues and trends that will affect how and whom nonprofit executives will manage for the year 2000 and beyond, with chapters on mission, strategic planning, marketing, public relations, fund raising, fiscal management, human resources management, communications, running productive meetings, governance, and volunteers. 238 pages.

Profiles of Excellence. By E. B. Knauft, Renee A. Berger, and Sandra T. Gray. Washington, D.C.: Independent Sector, 1990. Suggests how nonprofits can achieve excellence by applying four basic principles of outstanding nonprofit leadership. Draws on data reflecting experiences of more than one thousand U.S. nonprofit groups; includes ten detailed case studies. 197 pages. Order from Independent Sector.

Books Focused on One Function

Community Relations

Marketing Workbook for Nonprofits. By Gary J. Stern. St. Paul: Amherst H. Wilder Foundation, 1990. Provides instruction, nonprofit case studies, and six step-by-step worksheets that guide the user through each stage of the marketing process. 132 pages. Order from Wilder Foundation.

Financial

Accounting and Budgeting in Public and Nonprofit Organizations: A Manager's Guide. By C. Y. M. Garner. San Francisco: Jossey-Bass Publishers, 1991. 272 pages.

Accounting for Contributions and Financial Statement Display: Important Developments for Not-for-Profit Organizations and Their Boards. By Ernst & Young, 1994. Covers the 1993 rules (FASB Statements 116 and 117) issued by the Financial Accounting Standards Board. Provides overview of the new accounting rules for nonprofits, including alternative approaches, and implementation issues. 27 pages. Request from local Ernst & Young office.

Financial and Accounting Guide for Not-for-Profit Organizations (fifth edition). By Malvern J. Gross, Jr., Richard F. Larkin, and William Warshauer, Jr. New York: John Wiley & Sons, 1995. 681 pages.

Sales Tax Exemptions for Charitable, Educational, and Religious Nonprofit Organizations. By Janne Gallagher. Washington, D.C.: Independent Sector, 1992. Provides a broad-brush look at the patterns of sales tax exemptions as they affect nonprofits in the course of carrying out their missions and related activities and fund raising. 16 pages.

Self-Help Accounting: A Guide for the Volunteer Treasurer. By John P. Dalsimer and Susan J. Ellis. Philadelphia: Energize Books, 1989. 100 pages.

Fund Raising

The Fund Raising Handbook. By Robert L. Krit; sponsored by the Society for Nonprofit Organizations. Dubuque, Iowa: Kendall/Hunt Publishing Company, 1993. 226 pages.

Program Planning and Proposal Writing. By Norton Kiritz. Los Angeles: The Grantsmanship Center, 1980. 48 pages. Order from the Grantsmanship Center.

See also the collection of the Foundation Center outlined in "Sources of Assistance."

Governance

The Board Members' Book (second edition). By Brian O'Connell. Washington, D.C.: Independent Sector, 1994. A practical guide to the essential functions of nonprofit boards of directors. 53 pages. Order from Independent Sector.

Planning

Strategic Planning Workbook for Nonprofit Organizations. By Bryan Barry. St. Paul: Amherst H. Wilder Foundation, 1986. Provides step-by-step instructions for developing sound, realistic strategic plans; approach can be tailored to any nonprofit organization. 88 pages. Order from Wilder Foundation.

Strategic Planning for Public and Nonprofit Organizations: A Guide to Strengthening and Sustaining Organizational Achievement. By John M. Bryson. San Francisco: Jossey-Bass Publishers, 1988. Explains a variety of approaches to help leaders and managers of public and nonprofit organizations fulfill their missions and satisfy their constituents through strategic planning. 302 pages.

Public Policy

Leadership for the Common Good: Tackling Public Problems in a Shared Power World. By John M. Bryson and Barbara C. Crosby. San Francisco: Jossey-Bass Publishers, 1992. Addresses dynamics of change in a shared-power, "no-one-in-charge" world, presenting a comprehensive, integrated approach to public leadership and how it can be used by nonprofit practitioners, community leaders in business, and government to tackle public problems. 414 pages.

Lobby? You? Washington, D.C.: Independent Sector, 1988. How-to guidelines for advancing your cause by letting your legislators know what you want and why it is needed. Encourages groups to come under 1976 U.S. Lobby Law. 12 pages. Order from Independent Sector.

The Nonprofit Lobby Guide: Advocating Your Cause and Getting Results. Washington, D.C.: Independent Sector, 1991. 48 pages. Order from Independent Sector.

Quality

Quality Improvement: Special Challenges for Human Services Nonprofits. Minneapolis: Center for Nonprofit Management, 1995. Summarizes what an innovative team of Minnesota nonprofit senior executives learned during a year studying the primary themes of quality improvement and how those themes and principles apply to nonprofit organizations (especially human service organizations). Outlines a quality improvement process for nonprofits. 15 pages. Order from CNM.

Quality Management in the Nonprofit World. By Larry W. Kennedy. San Francisco: Jossey-Bass Publishers, 1991. Discusses how managing for quality can not only improve the services that nonprofits provide, but also increase the number of people served. Outlines quality management techniques, training systems, and performance standards. 172 pages.

Risk Management

Am I Covered for . . . ? A Guide to Insurance for Nonprofits. By Mary Lai, Terry Chapman, and Elmer Steinbock. Washington, D.C.: Nonprofit Risk Management Center, 1992. 283 pages. Order from NRMC.

Child Abuse Prevention Primer for Your Organization. Washington, D.C.: Nonprofit Risk Management Center, 1995. 88 pages. Order from NRMC.

D&O—Yes or No? Directors & Officers Insurance for the Volunteer Board. Washington, D.C.: Nonprofit Risk Management Center, 1991. 20 pages. Order from NRMC.

Staff Screening Tool Kit: Keeping Bad Apples Out of Your Organization. Washington, D.C.: Nonprofit Risk Management Center, 1994. 116 pages. Order from NRMC.

Collaboration

Collaboration Handbook: Creating, Sustaining, and Enjoying the Journey. By Michael Winer and Karen Ray. St. Paul: Amherst H. Wilder Foundation, 1994. Offers tips to speed the collaborative journey, including worksheets, annotated resources, illustrations, case studies, and a number of examples. 192 pages. Order from Wilder Foundation.

Periodicals

Chronicle of Philanthropy, P.O. Box 1989, Marion, OH 43306. Biweekly paper that bills itself as the "Newspaper of the Nonprofit World." Reports on news affecting nonprofits, management matters, fund raising techniques, IRS regulations, corporate/foundation grants, and conferences. Annual subscription $67.50 (six months also available for $36).

Legal-Ease. Center for Nonprofit Management, University of St. Thomas, 52 Tenth St. S., Minneapolis, MN 55403. Quarterly, four-page newsletter sponsored by several nonprofit service organizations. Covers new federal and Minnesota state laws and regulations and related matters of prime interest to nonprofit managers and their boards. Free subscription to Minnesota-based nonprofits; $5 annually to others to cover printing and postage.

Nonprofit Management News. Center for Nonprofit Management, University of St. Thomas, 52 Tenth St. S., Minneapolis, MN 55403. Quarterly, four-page newsletter that focuses on nonprofit management issues, developments, tools, new management-related research, and best practices. Free subscription to Minnesota-based nonprofits; $5 annually to others to cover printing and postage.

Nonprofit Times. Davis Information Group, 190 Tamarack Circle, Skillman, NJ 08558. Monthly in tabloid format. Covers legislative and regulatory issues affecting nonprofits as well as fund raising, marketing, and other management practices and tips. Annual subscription $59; free to "qualified, full-time nonprofit executives who specify job title and responsibilities and annual gross revenues over $500,000."

Nonprofit World. The Society for Nonprofit Organizations, 6314 Odana Rd., Suite 1, Madison, WI 53719. Bimonthly magazine. Focuses on leadership and nonprofit management. Annual subscription $79; free to members of the Society ($95 annual membership fee).

Addresses for Ordering Books Not Available through Bookstores

Amherst H. Wilder Foundation, Publication Center, 919 Lafond Ave., St. Paul, MN 55104

Center for Nonprofit Management, 52 Tenth St. S., Minneapolis, MN 55403

Foundation Center, 79 Fifth Ave., New York, NY 10007

Grantsmanship Center, P.O. Box 17220, Los Angeles, CA 90017

Independent Sector, 1828 L St. NW, Washington, DC 20036

KMPG Peat Marwick, 345 Park Ave., New York, NY 10154

Nonprofit Risk Management Center, 1001 Connecticut Ave. NW, Suite 900, Washington, DC 20036

Index

Joan M. Hummel has extensive communications experience, with a focus on public relations and marketing communications for nonprofit organizations and government agencies. She has served as both staff and board member at nonprofit organizations, and has experience in working with foundations and other supporters of nonprofit organizations.

The Center for Nonprofit Management is based in the Graduate School of Business, University of St. Thomas, Minneapolis-St. Paul. It develops and offers management development courses, informational services, and management tools to improve the organizational effectiveness of nonprofit organizations. The Center's programs are designed to meet the specific and special needs of nonprofit managers and other professionals.